CHROOT YO...
RED HAT/CENT...
EXTREME HARDENING

redhat.

CentOS

NetSec
NETWORK SECURITY
The Security Your Network Needs

Renato Oliveira

How to harden your Linux Servers (Red Hat/Centos 8)
The Complete Guide
By Renato de Oliveira

About the Author

I have been working in IT since 1992, and I have been through most IT positions. I started controlling stock and typing data into the computer. When I remember I did not even know what a computer was. I thought the Computer was the monitor alone. The first computer I worked with was a PC 286 with a 15MHz and turbo button, which if pressed, would display 25MHz. I had 256K of RAM and 32M of a hard disk, that was a super-fast computer, and I had to clean the hard disk every three months. I was running MS-DOS 5.5 and Windows 3.1.

In 1994 I had my first contact with the Internet (nothing like what it is today). I used a 33k Modem to connect to the Internet. That was when the three major players had their private Networks; Microsoft with `MSN`, `AOL,` and `Compuserve`.
I connect to Microsoft Networks, and I managed to run a scary phone bill. I loved that noise the modem makes when connecting. I miss it!

I also remember I said to my boss at the time, let's make use of the Internet (in 1994), and my boss said; "we sell clothes we don't need the Internet!" I find it funny when I remember this.

I learned how to fix and build PCs, I learned how to set up LANs (Local Area Networks), and I learned Linux. I started by having to download the "boot image", IDE or SCSI, then I had to download the "root image". It was a nightmare. The first Linux distribution I came across was the Conectiva Linux and right after Red hat 5.1 (this before Red Hat became Enterprise and its last free version was 9.0). That was a time when "`IPForward`" was used to set up firewall rules.

In 1997 I had an idea of setting up a company to develop a ready to use Network KIT, based on `Plug'n'Play`. The kit would contain a Switch and Network Cards compatible with Windows and could auto-install necessary drivers and would auto set IPs in the same range. I never put this idea to practice and regret very much.

I learned Windows NT 4.0, and I have to say; I liked it a lot. Security those days were pretty much inexistent.

Things were pretty slow indeed, to download a 5Mbyte MP3 using a 33K modem, it would take 5-10 hours, and I used to sit patiently waiting.
The Internet was pretty much static, with pages in HTML, then DHTML came about, and things started to get more interesting.

There were many cool browsers, such as Netscape Navigator, Microsoft decided to get into the arena, and I saw Internet Explorer 2.0. I still preferred Netscape; it was nicer and had many more exciting features.

In 1998 I managed to migrate a full Windows NT network to Linux; that was a challenge and gave me a lot of knowledge, and it was a lot of fun. I think I set up around 100 Computers between Servers and Clients.

The Internet has changed, Linux has changed, Networks have become more complex, and we can do so many more things now a day, since Online Banking, shopping, pay bills, book tickets, trips, and flights. It is amazing how the Internet developed and scaled, I would say; very quickly. So while the Internet has evolved and grew so did our concerns and the need for security. If you plug your PC right now in the UK, it can be accessed right away in Brazil pretty much by anyone. If you are responsible for a network and it is directly connected to the Internet, you need to secure it very well and take the measures I will describe within this book, to make sure it won't be compromised easily.

You see on the news all the time, big organizations have suffered from Cyber Attacks ranging from Data Breach/leak or DDOS (Distributed Denial of Service.

It is fundamental to have a security policy and implement it; it is better to be safe than sorry—two things which can be very difficult to recover: Data and reputation.

4

Taking the correct approach can prevent a lot of bad things from happening. Even if you suffer from an attack and get compromised, you can still delay it, detect it, and recover from it in good time, either by isolating the compromised system or by restoring the lost data.

Remember, there is no silver bullet! Cyber Security is a constant battle of monitoring, checking logs, scanning the network, segmenting the system, setting up isolation zones etc.

Keep your eyes open and always be proactive; don't leave any stone unturned. Train your users and your IT team, in understanding the risks, including when socializing, so they do not disclose important information. Many attackers use Social Engineering to gain trust from users and then getting hold of valuable information. I am not going to talk about Social Engineering in this book; there are many good books available already.

This book focuses on server security. I hope you read it, enjoy it, and make use of it.

Acknowledgement

I always loved writing, if I write well, well, this is another matter. I wrote this book because I want to contribute with the Linux community and make sure I pass along all the great things I've learned along all these years about Linux, by reading, researching and just playing with it.

I started learning Linux because of a project I had in my hands, migrate 100 Windows NT 4.0 to Linux, to save the cost with Microsoft Licenses.

I believe I started learning IT a bit late, I was 18 years old, but it was a significant change in my life, and I thank Paul Ashton (my first boss), he believed in my potential and offered me to start working with computers by controlling the shop stock. From there in I learned everything by myself.

I thank my mother she paid a course for me back in 1996 on how to build and troubleshoot PCs. I already knew quite a lot, but I want to refine my technique and also exchange ideas.

I always admired people who know more than I do; this gives me the strength to learn more and become as good as them. There two people who inspired while I was learning IT; a Guy who sold computers for the companies I worked for, he knew a lot about hardware and that pushed me to learn more and more.

There was also the guy who was my teacher when I was doing the course on how to build PCs; he knew a lot about UNIX, LAN, and PCs. Some people in our lives give us the force to go beyond and reach to places where we never envisaged; we would achieve.

I also have to acknowledge to myself; I am determined to learn and improve my skills. Against all the odds, I am here and learned a lot about many things.

Chroot your Red Hat/Centos Server Extreme Hardening

This book focuses its attention on securing your Linux server. Linux has become one of the most used Operating system, if not the most used, across the world and all over the Internet.

Most web servers run on `Apache` and `Linux`, a lot of `MTAs` also run Postfix or `Sendmail` and they both run on `Linux`. With the advent of broadband, more and more home users are setting up their web servers and leaving it always connected to the Internet.

A few years ago (about 15) years, I had set up a `Linux` router for my Internet at home, I left the default configuration, just because a) I did not want to spend too much time making it secure (I did not think anyone would have an interest in my router) b) I was lazy c) I did not care much. So the story goes, my Internet became slow, and I started to investigate the issue. I managed to track the slowness to my `Linux` router; it had been targeted, by multiple requests and attempts to break in, trying the root password. I examined the /var/log/messages log, and there were 200000 failed attempts to log in to my router, which sparked my desire to become an expert in Cyber Security, this is to show that we all need to take security seriously.

There are so many different aspects of security, and I will try to cover most of them. If you take it seriously, you will try and implement most of my recommendations if not all; your server is exposed, and connected to the Internet is a constant danger.

A considerable amount of exploits and vulnerabilities are discovered on a daily basis. As soon as a new vulnerability is found, it gets used right away by hackers.

I believe we all have responsibilities with our security, also with our customers, to the company we work for, etc. etc.

This book is about Linux Security, but its ideas within will be helpful to protect almost any server or operating system.

As you probably have seen on TV and news, pretty much daily we hear or see different stories; compromised servers, scammed users and companies losing customer data and so many horrible things.

While there is no such thing as a silver bullet, we can certainly do a lot to make it harder for cybercriminals to gain access to our Linux servers. It is our responsibility to lock every single door we can think of and keep our eye open to logs and any unusual behaviour of our servers.

A lot of this information you can find online, but I am writing it organized in a way which is specific to make our Linux servers, more secure from the physical aspect to the OS, to the admin tasks and some applications.

I am going to describe each section, talk about reasons and tell you which settings to adjust and show you how to set them up. I will try and explain each configuration setting.

I think security is a fascinating subject, and we need to be more aware of what we can do to improve it. There are so many aspects, but it is essential to raise barriers, the more, the better.

This book covers a lot of aspects of Linux security, if you follow it through, your server will become much more secure, and you should have fewer issues with it or them.

This book does not cover network design security, networking, or network segmentation. This book is about Linux security.

I think you won't be disappointed in buying this book, we covered a lot of ground and put a lot of effort in making it as accurate as possible, and covering as many aspects as possible.

Index

Physical

- ➢ **Physically Securing your server**
- ➢ **RFID**
- ➢ **Monitoring Cameras**
- ➢ **Lock server Room**
- ➢ **Lock racks**
- ➢ **Lock server's case**
- ➢ **Secure the server to the rack**
- ➢ **BIOS**
  - ○ **Disable CDROM**
  - ○ **Disable USB Access**
  - ○ **NIC (Network Interface Cards)**
  - ○ **Power Supply**
  - ○ **ILO or DRAC Interface**
  - ○ **Hard Disk**

Operating System

- • **Set boot password for Grub**
- • **Protect against single-user mode**
- • **Locking down single-user mode**
- • **Disable Interactive Hotkey Start-up at Boot**
- • **Create separate partitions for each file system**
- • **Mount /boot partition as read-only**
- • **Mount /sbin partition as read-only**
- • **Mount /var and /var/tmp partitions with options (nodev,nosuid,noexec)**

- Secure even further the /tmp partition
- Secure /proc file system
- Disable <Ctrl>+<Alt>+<Delete>
- Disable unnecessary services
- Set /etc/aliases file
- Modify files /etc/issue, /etc/issue.net and /etc/motd
- Configure /etc/host.conf file
- Use TCP-Wrappers
- Configure the /etc/cron.deny and /etc/at.conf files
- Secure Linux Virtual Terminals (TTYs)
- Configure Syslog Server
- Server Firewall (IPTables)
- Keep your system slim
- Don't install X window
- Secure your Network TCP/IP stack
- Set Date and Time

Applications

- SSH Security
- Web Servers
- FTP Security
- SFTP (mysftp shell)
- Email Security

Sysadmin

- Security Policy
- Don't log as root
- Enable automatic log out

- **Disabling root SSH logins**
- **Lock important config files**
- **LOCK MAC address**

Accounts

- **Burry the root password**
- **Using Sudo**
- **Host-Based Intrusion Detection System**
- **Some Important OSSEC Features**
- **OSSEC Installation**
- **Get Rid of Offenders**
- **Fail2ban**
- **SELinux**
- **Keep your system updated**
- **Automate Updates**
- **Backups**
- **Subscribe to Security Alerts**

Monitoring

- **Monitoring your Server**
- **Shell Commands**
- **Rotate your logs**
- **Audit Log**
- **Monitor Your Logs**
- **Install Log watch**
- **Install Log watch**
- **Nagios**
- **Installing Nagios NRPE**

- **Graphing trends**

Encryption

- **Encryption**
- **Configuring Apache to use SSL with a Self-Signed Certificate**
- **SSH**
- **VPNs**
- **Dormant Data**

HOWTOs

- **How to install Grafana**
- **Miscellaneous**
- **How To Disable Local Login for specific users**
- **How To Install Nagios using Yum**
- **How to check if Your Domain is blacklisted**
- **Apache Access Log**
- **How to Set-up Spam Assassin**
- **How To Install and Configure ClamAV**
- **How To Add TLS Support to Postfix**
- **HOW TO SSH Port Knocking**

Glossary

Physical

The first line of defence is physical or Layer 1 of the OSI model, if anyone can get hold physically of any of your servers, it is game over. I cannot emphasize enough how important it is to protect your servers physically. What good is having firewalls, `IDP/IDS` if anyone can quickly gain access to your servers? What can anyone do physically do damage your servers or compromise them? A lot!

It is important to note that; physical security is to protect everyone and everything! It protects your data, your equipment, your systems, your facilities and company assets; being hardware or employees.

There are many ways in which we can use physical security to protect our most valuable assets:
- by planning and designing a security layout,
- by using environmental components,
- by having a plan for emergency response,
- by training users and your IT staff,
- by implementing access control,
- by setting up an intrusion detection system,
- by having power and fire protection systems in place.
- by having a BCP (Business Continuity Plan)
- by having disaster and recovery policies
  Some are very important to reduce business interruption by natural disasters, sabotage or even in the event of an explosion.

It is essential to have multiple security controls in places to make it more challenging for attackers to gain control of valuable company resources, i.e. Servers.

I believe an excellent approach is creating a very comprehensive protection system by breaking it down into layers and protecting each layer accordingly. If an attacker compromises one of the layers, he/she will still have to break in the additional layers to obtain full control of your servers. The idea is more or less like a castle, with a moat and strong and high walls, watched by guards and a single gate being controlled and monitored at all times.

I call this the triple 'D': Delay, Detection and Denial, these are controls used for securing the environment where your systems reside. Attempts to obtain physical access should be "**Delayed**" by using fences, gates, and guards around the building. By using locked doors and security vaults, we are protecting our physical equipment's the use of "**Denial**". Then the next line of defence is to use a Physical Intrusion Detection Systems (IDS) coupled with alarms to notify if a breach is "**Detected**".

If an attacker manages to get through all lines of defence, then security measures such as a cable lock on a computer/laptop or server will delay further until the security team responds or the police arrive.

The triple 'D' (Delay, Detection and Denial) Security Approach help in preventing attackers from gaining control to critical resources, such as; administrative controls, building design, policies and much more.

Physical controls include but are not limited to; perimeter security, motion sensor detectors, and intrusion alarms. Technical controls include smart cards used for access control, physical security intrusion detection systems, guards and CCTV systems etc.

Physically Securing Your Server

Physically securing a server is a big task, don't kid yourself. There are many things to think and to take care of, so I have a comprehensive list of such things. You don't need to implement them all; there will be some recommendations, which you will have to judge the pros and cons and make the decision in implementing them or not. If it impacts your daily business operations, then you will have to compromise. Make sure your building is locked at all times, have security guards at reception or a receptionist, don't let any unknown person out of your sight and especially do not let them wander around alone.

I do not recommend plugging your server to the network, without preparing them first and giving at least a minimum of security.

RFID systems

Radio-frequency identification (RFID) – This is such a vital technology to use to secure your doors and guarantee they will remain locked at all times. This technology uses a proximity a card, previously provided by the company to employees or third-party companies, configured to only allow access to rooms where each user should have access. Never allow employees or third-party contractor's access to your servers, if they do not need to. Make sure the cards are tracked, logged and disabled in case of loss or if an employee leaves the company.

Remember, it is crucial only to allow authorized personnel to have access to your servers.

There are plenty of options and companies offering this service, and some are very secure and provides integration to the police, while others are more basic. Check which one is more appropriate for you and your budget.

Monitoring Cameras

It is essential to have cameras monitoring the surrounds of your building, the entrance 24/7 and of course, a team watching the cameras. Otherwise, what is the point in monitoring? You also need to back up these videos for posterior analysis.

Some areas to monitor are reception, corridors, each room separately, and especially you need to watch your server room:

Install cameras with motion sensor and night vision so you can see at night and in the dark. Cameras are cheap nowadays, so have more than one camera monitoring different angles.

- Monitor back and front of the Racks
- Monitor all doors (entrance and exit)
- Monitor corridors

Segment the network used to connect all cameras. Separate them from your corporate network and isolate it with VLAN and ACLs, only allow access to authorized users and members of the IT/Security team.

The point is to keep an eye on your assets and make sure your server room and servers are always under surveillance 24x7.

Lock the Server Room

Take care of your server room and protect it with **Radio-frequency identification (RFID).** Create zones, make the doors which give access to the server room part of a separate zone, and only give to access it, to authorised personnel. Ideally, you would want your door system to alert you of any breach attempt.

It is crucial to monitor such a system and keep your eyes open to breach attempts.

I strongly suggest writing a Security Policy, and any user who needs access to the server room must be approved and cleared by the security team or managers. Set is so access using the RFID tag also requires a PIN.

Lock the Racks

Each rack comes with front and back and also side panels; keep them closed and do not feel tempted to remove the doors or side panels. Some sysadmin finds those doors annoying. Make sure you add a keypad lock and only disclose the PIN to authorized personnel and IT team members or security team. The process should be incorporated into your Security Policy. Changing the PIN to open racks frequently is also important.

You have to make it challenging to get to your servers and also if an intruder made it to your server, it is difficult to reach it and get out of your building with it.

Locking server racks/cabinets are also part of this effort to secure them physically and creating a layered system, which slows down attackers, giving us time to react.

Lock the Server Case

Each server comes enclosed with a metal case, which can be left opened to allow access to its electronic components, such as; memory, CPU, Hard Disks etc. It is highly recommended you keep your server with its lead on and lock it with its key.

Typically most servers come with a key which one can use to lock it and make sure no one can have access to its internal components. If a malicious person can have access to the server components, they can do a lot of damage. Not so long ago, RAM was very expensive, and they used to get stolen by criminals, to sell them and make a bit of cash.

The BIOS Inside the case, is connected to the motherboard and that is what keeps BIOS settings (i.e. date/time), If you remove the battery, you will be erasing all the settings on your server BIOS and leaving them as default, without a password, for example.

Secure the Server to the rack

I highly recommend using Security Lock cable to attach the server to the rack/cabinet physically.

There isn't much to say about this. Some may say it is over the top, but I think it is better to be safe than sorry, especially if your servers are in a shared environment, which you don't have full control.

I don't think it causes any harm; it is cheap and can give you some extra peace of mind. So, it is a no brainer!

BIOS (Basic Input Output System)

Set a password to protect the BIOS and boot system. A password will prevent unauthorized access to the Operating system and the BIOS. This step is the first layer of protection for your server. If anyone gains physical access to your server, they will have to break the password; this will delay the attacker and give time for you to take action.

BIOS options to disable

- Set a boot password
- Set the BIOS access password
- Disable booting off USB
- Disable USB access
- Disable Serial interfaces

The drawback is; if you have to reboot the server remotely, you will need to do so using the ILO/DRAC, or some sort of remote console.

I believe it is well worth doing it, make sure you keep this in-line with your Security Policy and change the BIOS password frequently.

Some Sysadmins are complacent and don't even bother with this security measure, but it is one so cheap and easy to implement.
These settings will ultimately make your server more secure and make it harder for an intruder to get hold of it and compromise it.

It is crucial to keep the lead on and locked, if possible, with a key.

Disable or remove CD-ROM/DVD/Floppy Drive

Having a CD-ROM/DVD connected to your Server can be useful, but it can also be dangerous. If anyone can get hold physically of your server, it will be easy just to pop a CD or DVD into the drive and install whatever software they want, boot off a live Linux distro CD/DVD and control your server completely.

Disable USB access

The USB ports have the same potential, if not a more significant, to open up your servers for multiple attacks. One can plug a USB memory stick or USB drive, and copy your data, load code into the memory, install malware, boot off a LIVE Linux distro and do a lot of damage to the server.

NIC (Network Interface Card)

NIC (Network Interface Card) is the interface which connects your server to the Network, by attaching it to a HUB, Switch or router.
Disable any unused NICs, if you don't need it for redundancy, just disable it.
Ideally, you would want to connect your NICs in pairs to make them resilient and redundant, in case of one of the NICs breaks or has a problem; you won't lose connectivity to your Network.

Another critical point here is, turn on MAC address Security or Port Security at the Switch level.

If you are thinking about redundancy/resiliency, then you will need to use a technology called teaming (Windows terminology) and Bonding (Linux terminology).

There are some NICs which support encryption, but they are very few. If this type of device takes off, I think it would be a dream; to encrypt the traffic straight from your network card.

There are some options on the market, take a look at them, play with them and see if they do the job for you and your business.

Power Supply and Power lead

Having multiple power supplies is a must for any production server, each one connected to a different power source, this is important for resilient/redundant reasons, but we can argue it is also essential for security reasons. Suppose an attacker pulls the plug or disrupt the power source which is attached to a single power supply, all is good (having multiple power supplies connected to different power sources), and the server will carry on working, you will be alerted, and can take care of the situation without interruption. I would go to the extra length and using cable ties to attach the leads to make it difficult for accidental interruptions or even malicious interruptions.

ILO and Drac Interface

The first thing is; to set the Administrator, or Root password set it hard to guess. Create administrative user accounts, and set the level of permissions for each IT team member.

Incorporate this to your Security Policy and make sure to change passwords regularly. Test access to the ILO periodically.

Having access to the ILO or DRAC it is like having access to the server console, so make it safe, Use HTTPs to allow access, disable unnecessary services. Set a separate network for ILO/Drac only and only allow access to authorised IT team members.

Services to Disable

- Telnet
- HTTP
- FTP

Note: Disable all unused services and especially the ones using clear-text, i.e. Telnet

Services to Enable

- SSH
- HTTPS

Note: Buy an an SSL Certificate for the HTTPs service.

Hard disks

There are pretty much three different technologies you can choose from; they are SATA, SAS, and SSD.

The important thing is; not having a single disk (which can lead to a single point of failure), this is a disaster waiting to happen.

RAID volumes are essential, while this in itself won't give you security, it will provide you with resiliency and redundancy.

Having more than a single disk is essential, at least RAID 1 with two disks (for OS) and RAID 10 for data, this will give you a level of protection in case of a single disk failure, but won't give you protection in case of a disk controller failure, or if both disks break. I am not going to go into more details about this topic because it is not the focus of this book. If you need a complete full proof solution, in terms of redundancy/resiliency you would need to look at server mirroring or a SAN (Storage Area Network), but this is out of the scope of this book.

Operating System

Linux is an Operating System, and it is the interfae between you and the applications. Linux is an Opensource operating system, but there are some commercial Linux distributions, which you can pay for a subscription fee and have access to support, patches, updates, and documentation. The Linux 'kernel' began its life developed by Linux Torvalds. Much later, it became a world project, being developed by many developers around the world and each developer contributing to; improving it, to correcting bugs, making it faster, more reliable and secure.

Linux derived from UNIX (some prefer to use the term Unix Like). The important thing is; it is a very robust and secure Operating System.
Bug and Security fixes become available almost instantly; many intelligent software engineers are looking at the code and contributing to it.

Some say Linux is a community it has become a way of life, and if you are a sysadmin or a security professional, you need to know it. It has become a standard for the Internet, and most the web servers are running one version or another of Linux. There are many Linux distributions, and some are focused on security, some focus their attention to the end-user and try to make the desktop more comfortable to use.

Linux is very versatile and can be used pretty much with any task. It is powerful, and you can tune it, and secure pretty much every single aspect of it. Of course, it does take time to learn and master all these aspects, so I am bringing to you a lot of these security aspects in this book, to save you time, effort and helping you in securing it as best as you can, to make it harder to become compromised.

We will cover from the boot process to file systems and applications running. We aim to make it harder using the same layered approach used in physical security.

The boot process has six stages in the old SysV (BIOS, MBR, Grub, Kernel, INIT, and Runlevel programs), and we will touch upon most of them. There are some changes with Redhat/Centos 8, which I will also cover, which uses 'systemd' currently.

The steps to boot RHEL/Centos8 are:

1. The computer's BIOS performs POST.
2. BIOS reads the MBR for the bootloader.
3. GRUB 2 bootloader loads the vmlinuz kernel image.
4. GRUB 2 extracts the contents of the initramfs image.
5. The kernel loads driver modules from initramfs.
6. Kernel starts the system's first process, systemd.
7. The systemd process takes over. It:

   - Reads configuration files from the /etc/systemd directory
   - Reads file linked by /etc/systemd/system/default.target
   - Brings the system to the state defined by the system target
   - Executes /etc/rc.local

What's New in Red Hat Enterprise Linux/Centos 8

Red Hat Enterprise Linux 8 was built with some important principals in mind, such as:
- Operational Consistency and Cloud foundation
- Kernel 4.18
- Based on Fedora 28
- Runs on Intel/AMD 64-bit CPUs etc

RHEL8 is an attempt to reduce complexity and comes with 10 years of support, repositories for the base OS and Applications, which gives a more flexible lifecycle, offering multiple versions for DBs, etc. It brings tunable DB profiles and ansible system roles which provides a standard interface. Some changes to the yum package manager, which is based on Dandifielf Yum (DNS), supporting modular content and much better performance. It brings Insights a tool which provides sysadmins with analytics, machine learning and automation controls and a session recording feature, which can and will record playback terminal sessions for security and training.

Security has been well improved and it brings Secure default flags and static code analysis. FIPS (Federation Information Processing Standars) mode has been made easier to activate, this can be used with eficacia to secure SSH and Apache. RHEL8 brings strong crypto policies for encryption, TLS 1.3 is now system wide, SELinux has been improved for controlling files and directories much better. Software ID tags which will help with software inventory.

As you can see Red Hat 8 is packed with really cool technologies, features and a much tighter security.

Restrict network connectivity while installing

When you start the installation for a new Red Hat Enterprise Linux 8 server, the server won't be up-to-date and therefore might contain vulnerabilities, for this reason it is a good idea to limit connection only to the closest necessary network zone.

The safest choice is the "no network" zone, which means to leave your server disconnected during the installation process. In some cases, a LAN or intranet connection is sufficient while the Internet connection will be very insecure. To follow the best security practices, choose the closest zone with your repository.

After Installation Has finished

Once the installation has complete successfully, you need to update the server right away and start its firewall:

```
[root@e-netsec ~]# yum update
[root@e-netsec ~]# systemctl start firewalld
[root@e-netsec ~]# systemctl enable firewalld
```

Cryptographic Policies

Red Hat 8 brings a system component which configures the core cryptographic subsystem called Crypto policies, they cover the following protocols: TLS, IPSec, SSH, DNSSec and Kerberos protocols. It comes with a small set of polocies pre-defined which a sysadmin can use.

The following are the policy levels:

- DEAFULT: The default system-wide cryptographic policy level offers secure settings for current threat models. It allows the TLS 1.2 and 1.3 protocols, as well as the IKEv2 and SSH2 protocols. The RSA keys and Diffie-Hellman parameters are accepted if they are at least 2048 bits long.

- LEGACY: This policy ensures maximum compatibility with Red Hat Enterprise Linux 5 and earlier; it is less secure due to an increased attack surface. In addition to the DEFAULT level algorithms and protocols, it includes support for the TLS 1.0 and 1.1 protocols. The algorithms DSA, 3DES, and RC4 are allowed, while RSA keys and Diffie-Hellman parameters are accepted if they are at least 1023 bits long.

- FUTURE: A conservative security level that is believed to withstand any near-term future attacks. This level does not allow the use of SHA-1 in signature algorithms. The RSA keys and Diffie-Hellman parameters are accepted if they are at least 3072 bits long.

- FIPS: A policy level that conforms with the FIPS140-2 requirements. This is used internally by the fips-mode-setup tool, which switches the RHEL system into FIPS mode.

To view the current Crypto Policy:

```
[root@e-netsec ~]# update-crypto-policies -show
DEFAULT
```

Change the DEFAULT Crypto policy:

```
[root@e-netsec ~]# update-crypto-policies -set FUTURE
```

Note: Restart your system to apply the policy.

Set boot password for Grub2

GRUB2 (short for GNU Grand Unified Bootloader 2) is a boot loader software part of the GNU Project. GRUB2 is the reference implementation of the Free Software Foundation's Multiboot Specification, which provides a user with the choice to boot one of multiple operating systems installed on a computer or select a specific kernel configuration available on a particular operating system's partitions.

GRUB2 is predominantly used for Unix-like systems. The GNU operating system uses GNU GRUB as its boot loader, as do most Linux distributions and the Solaris operating system on x86 systems, starting with the Solaris 10 1/06 release.

In order to make Linux and the boot process more secure, you will need to add a password to it. Every time your Linux server reboots or boots up, GRUB will ask you to type in the password, making this process much more secure and in order to gain access to the OS, anyone will have to type in the GRUB password.

How to protect Grub2 with a password:

I strongly advise you to make a backup of all files, before modifications.

1. To set a `grub2` boot password, do the following:
   o Edit the file `/etc/grub.d/10_linux` and remove: `--unrestricted`
     ```
     [root@e-netsec ~]#  sed -i "/^CLASS=/s/ --
     unrestricted//" /etc/grub.d/10_linux
     ```

   o Type the following command at the SHELL:
     ```
     [root@e-netsec ~]#  grub2-setpassword
     ```

   - Check if the content of the file: `/boot/grub2/user.cfg`
     ```
     [root@e-netsec ~]# cat /boot/grub2/user.cfg
     GRUB2_PASSWORD=grub.pbkdf2.sha512.10000.448A6AD0E
     BE17D050063B259468EBE2AFACB083D6A865EEF83E02853E4
     284925879BE1A0E81A95593BAC95FB2A5FB0D5C8ACAB72235
     C75F7F274B2E666D2EE9A.51D4000CA72B2D971CC56921ECE
     96E1743574AD3D04D19D9D22E32FB7DF63909E4D87E1457AB
     9DDF28DFE2CDA419F99C345B42B9DB9FC4895EA5630D1697A
     979
     ```

   - Reconfigure `grub2` with the command bellow:
     ```
     [root@e-netsec ~]# grub2-mkconfig -o
     /boot/grub2/grub.cfg
     ```

   - Reboot your server and test; you should see the following:
     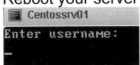

   - Enter the root username, hit ENTER, then type its password

2. Type in your password and, your server should start to boot.

Protect against single-user mode

Single user mode; is a mode in which a multi-user computer operating system boots to allow maintenance of the multi-user environments without any remote users connected.

Some tasks require exclusive access to shared resources. This mode can also be used for security purposes – to prevent networked services from running and allow the superuser to interact with the system, knowing no access over the network is taking place.

This mode can allow the sysadmin to recover a root lost password. We can simply switch to single-user mode, and the system will not ask for the root password, allowing the sysadmin to change it, without any restrictions, which is considered a massive security hole and this is what we will be fixing next.

I strongly advise you to make a backup of all files, before any modifications.

Locking down single-user mode

1. We need to generate a password for grub2, with e command below:
```
[root@e-netsec ~]# grub2-mkpasswd-pbkdf2
Enter password:
Reenter password:
PBKDF2 hash of your password is
grub.pbkdf2.sha512.10000.1300CB4DFC7DFC50D91368A8C7
7C739F92016E89AC881AD7A0D59BA2C8A9F9B1C72B91F2C9CF5
A4E58B5C0D4957C82A3229D3652B11CD6F4805B48F54D5B6860
```

```
.F6AE225B627BCA3ADFABC9C794EA363ED416BD89C05DD71E5B
7EEAD6B4FB69481D5FA256D2185616A4A00630484A9E6C9A891
4A51A0A42C9BCDEEA3BD0D2FFF3
```

2. Edit `/etc/grub.d/10_linux` file and at the bottom of the file add the following:

```
[root@e-netsec ~]# vi /etc/grub.d/10_linux
cat << EOF
set superusers="root"
password_pbkdf2 root
grub.pbkdf2.sha512.10000.1300CB4DFC7DFC50D91368A8C7
7C739F92016E89AC881AD7A0D59BA2C8A9F9B1C72B91F2C9CF5
A4E58B5C0D4957C82A3229D3652B11CD6F4805B48F54D5B6860
.F6AE225B627BCA3ADFABC9C794EA363ED416BD89C05DD71E5B
7EEAD6B4FB69481D5FA256D2185616A4A00630484A9E6C9A891
4A51A0A42C9BCDEEA3BD0D2FFF3
EOF
```

3. Save the file.
4. Make a backup of the original /boot/grub2/grub.cgf file:

```
[root@e-netsec ~]# cp -p /boot/grub2/grub.cfg
/boot/grub2/grub.cfg.orig.bak
```

5. Run the following command to set the password:

```
[root@e-netsec ~]# grub2-mkconfig -o
/boot/grub2/grub.cfg
```

6. Reboot your server and test editing the grub2 menu, it will ask you for the password.

Disable Interactive Hotkey Start-up at Boot

I strongly advise you to make a backup of all files, before any modifications.

Unlike RedHat 6.x, which had interactive mode startup enabled by default, this mode is disabled in RedHat 7/8 by default.

If you would like to enable interactive mode for RedHat 7/8 you need to append the following `system.config_spawn=true` to the kernel command-line in the bootloader.

It is a good move by RedHat disabling this by default.

Create separate partitions for each file system

Partitioning is a crucial part of implementing security at the file system level:

- o It limits the impact of a disk failure
- o It limits one partition from interfering to another, by overflowing.
- o It allows you to re-install Linux without losing your data.
- o It simplifies the process of creating backups
- o It allows administrators to add restrictions such as quotas and read-only permissions more effectively

I give a good starting point below, where we divide up the file system into multiple partitions/volumes. Each partition can be part of the same disk; can be a different disk all together or different arrays in different NASEs.

The important thing is; dividing your disk is wise and essential. Take some time thinking and planning how to divide the volumes in your server; this will give you a lot of peace of mind and improve your security, resiliency and recovery time.

Think for a moment if the `/tmp` partition is part of the `/` (root) filesystem, for example, and an application fills up the `/tmp` partition completely, this will affect the whole server. Any partition filling up has the potential to give you problems and bring your server down (denial of service). So monitoring your partitions is a key part of a security strategy. Monitoring is something I will talk about later, on Sysadmin tasks chapter.

- /usr
- /home
- /boot
- /var
- /var/tmp
- /tmp
- /sbin

Mount /boot partition as read-only

The /boot partition contains the kernel image and other files used during system start-up, i.e.: /boot/grub2/grub.conf, /boot/initramfs and /boot/vmlinuz files.

There are some partitions, such as /usr /sbin and /boot which can be mounted with the 'ro' (read-only) flag, which makes them read-only, as opposed to 'rw', (read/write). This option will lower the impact of rogue software or user mistakes and eliminates the need to use fsck on these partition after a power interruption or system crash.

It does, however, require a user to remount those partitions when they want to install programs or upgrade the kernel. Files that need to be accessed, such as; /etc/resolv.conf, we can move them to different directories, and a symlink created which points to their original location.

I strongly advise you to make a backup of all files, before any modifications.

```
[root@e-netsec~]# vi /etc/fstab <ENTER>
```

Add the following option ro (read-only)

```
/dev/sda1 /boot  ext3 ro,nosuid,nodev 0 0
```

Save the file and quit vi

Note: Whenever you need to update your system's kernel, you will need to make the boot partition `rw` (Read-Write) again.

Mount /sbin partition as read-only

The `/sbin` partition contains static and executable files or programs used for administrative tasks mainly used by root superuser.

There are some partitions, such as `/usr /sbin` and `/boot` can be mounted with the 'ro' (read-only) flag, which makes them `read-only`, as opposed to 'rw', (read/write). This option will lower the impact of rogue software or user mistakes and eliminates the need to use `fsck` on these partition after a power interruption or `system crash`.

It does, however, require a user to remount those partitions when they want to install programs or upgrade the `system`.

I strongly advise you to make a backup of all files, before any modifications.

```
[root@e-netsec~]# vi /etc/fstab <ENTER>
```

Add the following option ro (read-only)

```
/dev/sda3   /sbin  ext3    defaults,ro    1 2
```

Save the file and quit vi.

Note: Whenever you need to update your system's kernel, you will need to make the boot partition `rw` (Read-Write) again.

Mount /var and /var/tmp partitions with options (nodev, nosuid, noexec)

Whenever we are mounting ext2, ext3, and ext4 partitions, we can add a few security mount options to the /etc/fstab. The options are:

nosuid: This ignores the SUID bit and makes it just like an ordinary file.

noexec: This prevents the execution of files from partitions.

nodev: This ignores devices.

Bear in mind that; the options above can be circumvented by executing a non-direct path. Good news is; setting /tmp to noexec will stop a lot of exploits designed to be run directly from /tmp.

The nodev mount option specifies that the filesystem cannot contain special devices, i.e. block devices: This is a security measure. You don't want a filesystem which is accessible and writeable by any user, to allow the creation of character devices or access to random device hardware.

The nosuid mount option specifies that the filesystem cannot contain set userid files. Preventing setuid binaries on a world-writable filesystem makes sense because there's a risk of root escalation or other bad things here.

Note: I use these options in all my servers, but some folks only use them on public-facing servers where there are compliance considerations.

I strongly advise you to make a backup of all files, before any modifications.

```
[root@e-netsec~]# vi /etc/fstab <ENTER>
```

Add the following option `ro` (read-only)

```
/dev/sda4 /var/tmp ext3 ro,nosuid,nodev 0 2
/dev/sda5 /var ext3 relatime,nodev,nosuid,noexec 0 2
```

Save the file and quit vi.

Secure even further the /tmp partition

One of the reasons for making /tmp a separate partition or filesystem is to be able to mount it with the options `nosuid` and `noexec`. These options prevent privilege-escalation and arbitrary script execution from /tmp, respectively. These options are very useful in multi-user environments (e.g. hosting) where unprivileged users can have access to read/write data saved to /tmp but should not be able to perform either of these actions.

Another critical point is to be able to limit the amount of temporary data stored in /tmp (since not every application cleans up after itself) to prevent other more important partitions from filling up and causing service interruption and loss of data.

You may think this is over the top, but when it comes down to security, attackers can go crazy lengths to break into your system.

I strongly advise you to make a backup of all files, before any modifications.

1. Create a file size 512 MB for /tmp

```
[root@e-netsec~]# dd if=/dev/zero of=/var/TMP bs=1024
count=524288
```

2. Make it ext3
```
[root@e-netsec~]# mke2fs j /var/TMP
```

3. Backup the original /tmp
```
[root@e-netsec~]# mv  /tmp /tmp_backup
```

4. Create new /tmp folder
```
[root@e-netsec~]# mkdir /tmp
```

5. Mount the new temp file to /tmp
```
[root@e-netsec~]# mount -o loop,noexec,nosuid,rw
/var/TMP /tmp
```

6. Set Permission of /tmp
```
[root@e-netsec~]# chmod 1777 /tmp
```

7. Restore original /tmp and delete the Backup
```
[root@e-netsec~]# cp -R /tmp_backup/* /tmp/
[root@e-netsec~]# rm -rf /tmp_backup
```

```
8. [root@e-netsec~]# vi /etc/fstab <ENTER>
```

Add the line bellow:

```
9. /var/tmp /tmp ext4 rw,noexec,nosuid,nodev 0 0
```

Secure /proc file system

The /proc filesystem is a very special filesystem, and it is virtual. We sometimes call it a pseudo-filesystem. It doesn't contain 'real' files but just runtime system information, for example; system memory, mounted devices, hardware configuration and many more. We can think of it as a control and information centre for the kernel.

A lot of system utilities just make calls to files in the /proc filesystem. For example, lsmod is the same as running cat /proc/modules, while lspci is the same as running cat /proc/pci. You can change kernel parameters by just modifying files in the /proc while the system is running.

So how to make this so important file system more secure?
There are some parameters you can adjust to make things a little harder for an attacker. You can hide the Process ID for all other users, for example.

I strongly advise you to make a backup of all files, before any modifications.

See bellow a user can see every single PID:

```
[root@e-netsec~]# ls -ld /proc/[0-9]*
dr-xr-xr-x. 8 root     root     0 Dec 24 15:14 /proc/1
dr-xr-xr-x. 8 root     root     0 Dec 24 15:14 /proc/10
dr-xr-xr-x. 8 root     root     0 Dec 24 16:16 /proc/1016
dr-xr-xr-x. 8 root     root     0 Dec 24 15:14 /proc/1082

[root@e-netsec~]# vi /etc/fstab
```

Change the line below

From:
```
proc   /proc   proc     defaults    0 0
```

To:
```
proc   /proc   proc     defaults,hidepid=2    0 0
```

```
[root@e-netsec~]# su renato -
[root@e-netsec~]# $ ls -ld /proc/[0-9]*
```

Disable `<Ctrl>+<Alt>+<Delete>`

When we talk about production servers, it is a good idea to disable the `<Ctrl>+<Alt>+<Delete>` option, as this has the potential to disrupt your server, your applications and potentially corrupt your data and your filesystem.

By leaving this option enabled, you can open up your server for accidents and malicious attacks. I don't think it is a good idea to leave it configured and it won't do any harm by just disabling it.

I have seen time and time again; some sysadmins accidentally reboot servers.

So let's go ahead and disabled it.

I strongly advise you to make a backup of all files, before any modifications

```
RedHat/Centos 7 and 8 use the command systemctl to
accomplish this task
```

1. To disable `<Ctrl>+<Alt>+<Delete>` using `systemctl` follow the steps below:
   a. `[root@e-netsec~]# systemctl mask ctrl-alt-el.target`

   b. Edif the following file:
      `/etc/system/system.conf`
      `[root@centossrv01 systemd]# vi system.conf`
      `# See systemd-system.conf(5) for details.`

```
[Manager]
#LogLevel=info
#LogTarget=journal-or-kmsg
#LogColor=yes
#LogLocation=no
#DumpCore=yes
#CrashShell=no
#ShowStatus=yes
#CrashChVT=1
CtrlAltDelBurstAction=none
```

c. Save the file and exit vi.
d. Once you have saved the file, reload the configuration:
   `[root@e-netsec~]#systemctl daemon-reexec`

Note: I would advise doing this before you put your server to production and modifying this option during your maintenance window.

Disable unnecessary services

The rule when it comes down to security is; if you don't need it, don't install it, and don't leave it running. It is dangerous! It is a door which can be opened at any time and exploited.

Let's suppose we are setting up a web server; you will need Apache and all its dependencies. It is not necessary, for example, to install samba or telnet.

Understanding the purpose of your server and which services you will be deploying is a crucial factor. I would recommend not installing multiple services within the same server, for example, if you need a web server and a database server, I would advise splitting these two services into different servers. This way, you are reducing the attack surface for your server. It is easier to secure fewer services then multiple ones.

The Linux installer is pretty good and easy, but it also installs a lot of packages and services, if you are not careful.

Once the Linux installation has finished, and your server rebooted, check packages installed, and which services are running by default.

```
[root@e-netsec~]# yum list installed
```

```
[root@centossrv01 etc]# yum list installed
Loaded plugins: fastestmirror, langpacks
Loading mirror speeds from cached hostfile
 * base: mirror.freethought-internet.co.uk
 * extras: centos.mirrors.nublue.co.uk
 * updates: mirror.sov.uk.goscomb.net
base                                                |  3.6 kB      00:00
extras                                              |  2.9 kB      00:00
updates                                             |  2.9 kB      00:00
(1/4): base/7/x86_64/group_gz                       |  153 kB      00:00
(2/4): extras/7/x86_64/primary_db                   |  206 kB      00:01
(3/4): updates/7/x86_64/primary_db                  |  4.5 MB      00:02
(4/4): base/7/x86_64/primary_db                     |  6.1 MB      00:06
Installed Packages
GeoIP.x86_64                        1.5.0-14.el7                 @anaconda
NetworkManager.x86_64               1:1.18.4-3.el7               @anaconda
NetworkManager-libnm.x86_64         1:1.18.4-3.el7               @anaconda
NetworkManager-team.x86_64          1:1.18.4-3.el7               @anaconda
NetworkManager-tui.x86_64           1:1.18.4-3.el7               @anaconda
```

You also can use the command RPM:

```
[root@e-netsec~]# rpm -qa
```

```
[root@centossrv01 etc]# rpm -qa
openldap-2.4.44-21.el7_6.x86_64
setup-2.8.71-11.el7.noarch
gpgme-1.3.2-5.el7.x86_64
bind-license-9.11.4-16.P2.el7.noarch
passwd-0.79-6.el7.x86_64
kbd-misc-1.15.5-15.el7.noarch
bind-libs-9.11.4-16.P2.el7.x86_64
emacs-filesystem-24.3-23.el7.noarch
yum-3.4.3-167.el7.centos.noarch
nss-softokn-freebl-3.44.0-8.el7_7.x86_64
```

Remove unnecessary packages

```
[root@e-netsec~]# yum remove krb5-libs
```
for example

Check services running

```
[root@e-netsec~]# systemctl | grep -i running
```

```
[root@centossrv01 etc]# systemctl | grep -i running
session-1.scope                          loaded active running   Session 1 of user root
abrt-oops.service                        loaded active running   ABRT kernel log watcher
abrtd.service                            loaded active running   ABRT Automated Bug Reporting Tool
atd.service                              loaded active running   Job spooling tools
auditd.service                           loaded active running   Security Auditing Service
chronyd.service                          loaded active running   NTP client/server
crond.service                            loaded active running   Command Scheduler
dbus.service                             loaded active running   D-Bus System Message Bus
firewalld.service                        loaded active running   firewalld - dynamic firewall daemon
getty@tty1.service                       loaded active running   Getty on tty1
libstoragemgmt.service                   loaded active running   libstoragemgmt plug-in server daemon
lvm2-lvmetad.service                     loaded active running   LVM2 metadata daemon
```

You can also use the following command:

```
[root@e-netsec~]# chkconfig --list
```

```
[root@centossrv01 etc]# chkconfig --list

Note: This output shows SysV services only and does not include native
      systemd services. SysV configuration data might be overridden by native
      systemd configuration.

      If you want to list systemd services use 'systemctl list-unit-files'.
      To see services enabled on particular target use
      'systemctl list-dependencies [target]'.

netconsole      0:off   1:off   2:off   3:off   4:off   5:off   6:off
network         0:off   1:off   2:on    3:on    4:on    5:on    6:off
```

To disable Services

```
[root@e-netsec~]# systemctl | grep -i active | grep -I
running
```

```
[root@centossrv01 etc]# systemctl | grep -i active | grep -i running
session-1.scope                          loaded active running   Session 1 of user root
abrt-oops.service                        loaded active running   ABRT kernel log watcher
abrtd.service                            loaded active running   ABRT Automated Bug Reporting Tool
atd.service                              loaded active running   Job spooling tools
auditd.service                           loaded active running   Security Auditing Service
chronyd.service                          loaded active running   NTP client/server
crond.service                            loaded active running   Command Scheduler
dbus.service                             loaded active running   D-Bus System Message Bus
firewalld.service                        loaded active running   firewalld - dynamic firewall daemon
getty@tty1.service                       loaded active running   Getty on tty1
libstoragemgmt.service                   loaded active running   libstoragemgmt plug-in server daemon
lvm2-lvmetad.service                     loaded active running   LVM2 metadata daemon
NetworkManager.service                   loaded active running   Network Manager
polkit.service                           loaded active running   Authorization Manager
postfix.service                          loaded active running   Postfix Mail Transport Agent
rngd.service                             loaded active running   Hardware RNG Entropy Gatherer Daemon
rpcbind.service                          loaded active running   RPC bind service
rsyslog.service                          loaded active running   System Logging Service
smartd.service                           loaded active running   Self Monitoring and Reporting Technology (SMART) Daemon
sshd.service                             loaded active running   OpenSSH server daemon
systemd-journald.service                 loaded active running   Journal Service
systemd-logind.service                   loaded active running   Login Service
```

To prevent a service from starting at boot time, use te following command:

```
[root@e-netsec~]# systemctl disable rpcbind.service
```

To stop a service, use the following command:
```
[root@e-netsec~]# systemctl stop rpcbind.service
```

To remove a package, use the following command:
```
[root@e-netsec~]# rpm -qa | grep rpcbind
```

Remove package
```
[root@e-netsec~]#  yum remove rpcbind
```

Note: These are just examples, you need to assess your server, and decide which services are essential, and which ones you must disable.

Set /etc/aliases file

In terms of security /etc/aliases file won't offer much, but we need to monitor what is going on in our servers. A good practice is to; set majority of aliases to send emails to the root user, and then set the root user to forward all emails to a monitored inbox, i.e. sysadmin, for example.

The /etc/aliases file is part of Sendmail package, which is an MTA (Mail Transfer Agent). This file sets which accounts e-mails should be forwarded to once receive by an alias, and the root's emails should be sent to a security team mailbox.

E-mails can also be piped to programs or can be directed into a file. All e-mails from the user "e-netsec" would be sent to /dev/null (also known as "black hole")

```
e-netsec:/dev/null
```

Changes made to the file `/etc/aliases` do not take effect until the `newaliases` command is executed to build `/etc/aliases.db`.

I strongly advise you to make a backup of all files, before any modifications.

```
[root@e-netsec~]# vi /etc/aliases
```

At the bottom of the file, add the line: `root: sysadmin@e-netsec.net`

```
mailer-daemon: postmaster
postmaster: root
nobody: root
hostmaster: root
webmaster: root
www: root
abuse: root
security: root
root: sysadmin@e-netsec.net

[root@e-netsec~]# newaliases
```

Modify the file `/etc/issue`, `/etc/issue.net` and `/etc/motd`

These three files they do not offer any security whatsoever, but it is advisable to configure them and add a warning message.

Since the publication of the "Computer Misuse Act 1990," it has been strongly recommended that servers have configured a banner before allowing access to users. The Act says; it is an offence of unauthorized access can only be committed if the offender knew at the time that the access he intended to obtain was unauthorized. Login banners are the best way to achieve this. The "Regulation of Investigatory Powers Act 2000" also requires information to be given to computer users: login banners may also be an excellent way to do this dissemination.

I strongly advise you to make a backup of all files, before any modifications.

```
[root@e-netsec~]# vi /etc/issue
```

Add the message below, save the file and quit

═══

This system is for the use of authorized personnel only. This system is monitored, and any attempt to access it will be logged and fully investigated, by checking the source IP address.

Anyone using this system expressly consents to such monitoring and is advised that if such monitoring reveals possible evidence of criminal activity, we will provide the evidence from such monitoring to the police.

═══

```
[root@e-netsec~]# cp /etc/issue /etc/issue.net

[root@e-netsec~]# cp /etc/issue /etc/motd
```

Configure /etc/host.conf file

Configuring this file doesn't give much security, but I believe that the more barriers and checks we put in place, the harder it will become for the majority of the attackers. If we can at least defeat some of these hackers wannabes, then we are in the right place.

Some people agree, some people will disagree, but we should not leave any unturned stone. So let's set it up!

This file specifies how name resolution happens. Linux uses a resolver library to obtain the IP address corresponding to a hostname. Following is a sample /etc/host.conf file:

I strongly advise you to make a backup of all files, before any modifications.

```
[root@e-netsec~]# vi /etc/host.conf
```

Add the lines below, save and quit the file

Lookup names via DNS first then fall back to /etc/hosts.
```
order bind,hosts
```

We have machines with multiple addresses.
```
multi on
```

Check for IP address spoofing.
```
nospoof on
```

The "*order*" option indicates the order of services. This entry specifies that the resolver library should first consult the name server to resolve a name and then check the /etc/hosts file. A recommendation is to set the resolver library to check first the name server, then the /etc/hosts file (hosts).

The "*multi*" option determines whether a host in the /etc/hosts file can have multiple IP addresses and multiple NICs.If you have a multihomed Server, then this option should be set to ON.

The '*nospoof*' option is to not allow spoofing on this machine. IP-Spoofing is a security exploit. In this type of attack, a device looks like a legitimate server. Set this option to ON.

Use TCP-Wrappers

To have control over network services access, is an essential security task which all security professionals face. Linux has quite a few tools which work well. We have *iptables* (*iptables* is deprecated in RHLE 8), `Firewalld and nftables` are the most recent tools to configure packet-filtering rules used by the Linux kernel.

For many network services, TCP wrappers add an extra layer of protection and security by specifying which hosts are allowed or not to connect to "wrapped" network services.
See a picture diagram below:

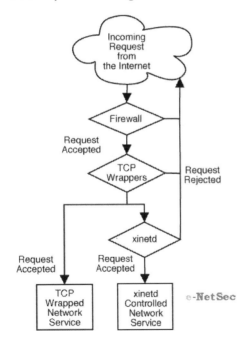

The TCP wrappers package (`tcp_wrappers`) is installed on the system by default.

When there is an attempt to connect to a TCP wrapped service; the service first checks the hosts access files (/etc/hosts.allow and /etc/hosts.deny) to determine if the client host is allowed to connect or not, It 'yes', then it uses the Syslog service to log the name of the source host and the destination service to /var/log/secure or /var/log/messages.

If a requesting client host is allowed to connect, TCP wrappers pass control of the connection to the destination service.

TCP wrappers is an essential tool to any server administrator's security chainset, most network services within Red Hat Enterprise/Centos use libwrap.a library, for example, ssh, Sendmail, and Xinetd (xinetd is deprecated).

I strongly advise you to make a backup of all files, before any modifications.

[root@e-netsec~]# vi /etc/hosts.allow

sshd: e-netsec.net # this allows all hosts in the domain e-netsec.net

[root@e-netsec~]# vi /etc/hosts.deny

vsftpd : .e-netsec.net # this allows all hosts in the domain e-netsec.net

Note: /etc/hosts.allow is checked first, if an entry is found, it won't check /etc/hosts.deny.

Configure the /etc/cron.deny and /etc/at.conf files

The cron and at services allow users to schedule commands to run at a specified time and date. It is possible to restrict these services to be used by particular users, i.e. roo and usr1, for example, while denying others, for instance, usr2. It is also possible to restrict user02 to run a script only, and not modify it or install a new one.

The *cron* service is present in almost all Linux/UNIX, and it performs individual admin or maintenance tasks. Both *cron* and *anacron* files make use of some configuration files and folders, store under /etc. Ordinary users can change and install their *cron* jobs, but not jobs by other users.

Add users who are allowed to use *cron* service.
/etc/cron.allow

Add users who are allowed to use at service.
/etc/at.allow

If both files /etc/cron.allow and /etc/at.allow do exist, and if the corresponding files /etc/cron.deny and /etc/at.deny do not exist, only users listed in the relevant allow files can run the crontab and at commands to schedule tasks.

Restrict at and cron to authorized users only

I strongly advise you to make a backup of all files, before any modifications.

1. First, delete /etc/cron.deny and /etc/at.deny files.
[root@e-netsec~]# rm /etc/cron.deny /etc/at.deny

2. Edit the file /etc/cron.allow

Add each user who is allowed to use the crontab and at

[root@e-netsec~]# vi /etc/cron.allow

e-netsec
root

[root@e-netsec~]# vi /etc/at.allow

Secure Linux Virtual Terminals (TTYs)

The /etc/securetty file allows you to specify which TTY devices the root superuser is allowed to use to login. The /etc/securetty file is read by the login program /bin/login. If the file /etc/securetty does not exist,the root user can log in using any communication device on the system, using the console or any network interface.

This file contains a list of the tty devices which the root user is allowed to log in, commented outlines means root login is not allowed.

Securetty is now disabled by default on RHEL8

The Dynamic nature of tty device files on modern Linux systems, the securetty PAM module has been disabled by default and the /etc/securetty configuration file is no longer included in RHEL.

Since /etc/securetty listed many possible devices so that the practical effect in most cases was to allow by default, this change has only a minor impact. However, if you need a more strict configuration, you have to add a line enabling the pam_securetty.so module to the appropriate files in the /etc/pam.d directory and create a new /etc/securetty file.

By default RHLE8 /etc/securetty file only allows the root user to log in at the console physically attached to the server. To make it even harder, create an empty file.

I strongly advise you to make a backup of all files, before any modifications.

```
[root@e-netsec~]# touch /etc/securetty
```

To prevent root user from log in using KDM, GDM and XDM add the following line:

```
auth [user_unknown=ignore success=ok ignore=ignore
default=bad] pam_securetty.so
```

To the following files:

```
/etc/pam.d/gdm
/etc/pam.d/gdm-autologin
/etc/pam.d/gdm-fingerprint
/etc/pam.d/gdm-password
/etc/pam.d/gdm-smartcard
/etc/pam.d/kdm
/etc/pam.d/kdm-np
/etc/pam.d/xdm
```

Configure Syslog Server

Servers and devices generate data and save it to disk; this data is known as "Logs". Logs are messages which contain essential information about many aspects of the server/device, such as; error events, kernel problems, security messages, login failure, and many more.

For example, a server running an SSH server can send messages about users logging on, while a web server can log 403 and a Firewall can send logs about policy denied, etc.

To make sure that logs from various servers and equipment in your network are recorded centrally on a logging server, we need to configure a Rsyslog server.

With RHEL8 Rsyslog works together with the system-journal service to provide local and remote logging support. Rsyslog server keeps reading syslog messages received by the system-journal service from the journal.rsyslogd and processes these sysogs events, saves them to files or forwards them to another server or service.

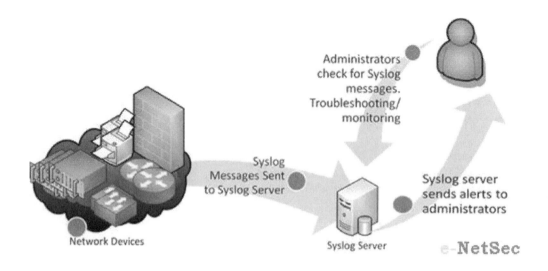

Why do we care about these logs? Because they are an essential source of information and can help in many ways, such as; troubleshooting problems, or troubleshooting a security event or attempt to break in and correlate events.

By maintaining such logs stored on the local server only, we have the risk of; if the server becomes compromised by an attacker, we won't be able to rely on those logs as they will probably be compromised.

I am not going to show how to set up the Syslog server, only how to set up your Linux server to forward Syslog messages to a remote Syslog Server. By forwarding the `syslog` messages to another server, your logs will be safe, and you will be able to troll through any time you want.

I strongly advise you to make a backup of all files, before any modifications.

1. Install Syslog Server
   ```
   [root@e-netsec~]# yum install syslog
   ```

2. **Edit the** `syslog.conf` **file**
   `[root@e-netsec~]# vi /etc/syslog.conf`

As an example add the line below to your `syslog.conf`
`user.* @10.0.0.100`

`Note: The configuration takes the form of:`
`<event>.* @ [ server IP],` **see the full** `rcsyslog.conf`
below:

`#$UDPServerRun 514`

`# Provides TCP syslog reception`
`#$ModLoad imtcp`
`#$InputTCPServerRun 514`

`#### GLOBAL DIRECTIVES ####`

`# Use default timestamp format`
`$ActionFileDefaultTemplate`
`RSYSLOG_TraditionalFileFormat`

`# File syncing capability is disabled by default.`
`This feature is usually not required,`
`# not useful and an extreme performance hit`
`#$ActionFileEnableSync on`

`# Include all config files in /etc/rsyslog.d/`
`$IncludeConfig /etc/rsyslog.d/*.conf`

`#### RULES ####`

`# Log all kernel messages to the console.`
`# Logging much else clutters up the screen.`
`#kern.*`
`/dev/console`

```
# Log anything (except mail) of level info or
higher.
# Don't log private authentication messages!
*.info;mail.none;authpriv.none;cron.none
/var/log/messages

# The authpriv file has restricted access.
authpriv.*
/var/log/secure

# Log all the mail messages in one place.
mail.*
-/var/log/maillog


# Log cron stuff
cron.*
/var/log/cron

# Everybody gets emergency messages
*.emerg
*

# Save news errors of level crit and higher in a
special file.
uucp,news.crit
/var/log/spooler

# Save boot messages also to boot.log
local7.*
/var/log/boot.log


# ### begin forwarding rule ###
# The statement between the begin ... end define a
SINGLE forwarding
# rule. They belong together, do NOT split them. If
you create multiple
# forwarding rules, duplicate the whole block!
```

```
# Remote Logging (we use TCP for reliable delivery)
#
# An on-disk queue is created for this action. If
the remote host is
# down, messages are spooled to disk and sent when
it is up again.
#$WorkDirectory /var/lib/rsyslog # where to place
spool files
#$ActionQueueFileName fwdRule1 # unique name prefix
for spool files
#$ActionQueueMaxDiskSpace 1g    # 1gb space limit
(use as much as possible)
#$ActionQueueSaveOnShutdown on # save messages to
disk on shutdown
#$ActionQueueType LinkedList    # run asynchronously
#$ActionResumeRetryCount -1     # infinite retries
if host is down
# remote host is: name/ip:port, e.g.
192.168.0.1:514, port optional
#*.* @@remote-host:514
user.* @10.0.0.100 # Line added
# ### end of the forwarding rule ###
```

Server Firewall

It is imperative to enable the server's Firewall, especially if you are going to place your server facing the public Internet. With a firewall ON and correctly configured, it is dangerous, without a firewall ON is suicidal. It is asking for trouble.

iptables is the package which contains the program used to configure the Linux kernel 2.4.x and later packet filtering framework. This software is used by sysadmins to configure the built-in Linux firewall. **NOTE**: IPTABBLES is deprecated in RHEL8.

Redhat 8 brings a new solution called `nftables` which is the new preferred way for configuring kernel firewall rules.

To install `nftables` onto your RHLE/Centos8 you will need the following packages:

- `nftables.x86_64`
- `libnftnl.x86_64`

```
[root@e-netsec~]# yum search nft
Loaded plugins: fastestmirror, langpacks
Loading mirror speeds from cached hostfile
 * base: mirror.freethought-internet.co.uk
 * extras: mirror.mhd.uk.as44574.net
 * updates: mirror.freethought-internet.co.uk
=============================== N/S matched: nft
==============================
libnftnl.i686 : Library for low-level interaction with
nftables Netlink's API
              : over libmnl
libnftnl.x86_64 : Library for low-level interaction with
nftables Netlink's API
              : over libmnl
libnftnl-devel.i686 : Development files for libnftnl
libnftnl-devel.x86_64 : Development files for libnftnl
nftables.x86_64 : Netfilter Tables userspace utillites

Name and summary matches only, use "search all" for
everything.
```

Install `nft` packge:
```
[root@e-netsec~]#  yum install nftables.x86_64 libnftnl.x86_64
libnftnl-devel.x86_64
```

Once the `nft` package has been installed, we can start using it
To check the ruleset
```
[root@e-netsec~]# nft list ruleset
```

To add a table:
```
[root@e-netsec~]#  nft list ruleset
[root@e-netsec~]#  nft add table inet my_table
```

```
[root@e-netsec~]# nft list ruleset
table inet my_table {
}
```

To create chains:

Chains are the objects that will contain firewall rules.

```
[root@e-netsec~]# nft add chain inet my_table my_filter_chain
{ type filter hook input priority 0\; }
```

To create rules (adding SSH and HTTP rules)

```
[root@e-netsec~]# nft add inet my_table my_filter_chain tcp
dport ssh accept
```

```
[root@e-netsec~]# nft add inet my_table my_filter_chain tcp
dport http accept
```

Listing new rules:

```
[root@e-netsec~]# nft add rule inet my_table my_filter_chain
tcp dport ssh accept
[root@centossrv01 sysconfig]# nft list ruleset
table inet my_table {
        chain my_filter_chain {
                type filter hook input priority 0; policy
accept;
                tcp dport http accept
                tcp dport ssh accept
        }
}
```

The nftables is much more flexible and powerful than iptables. I must say that nftables is both a userland uility and nft is a kernel subsystem, which builds upon the kernel's netfilter.

Keep your system slim

Don't install unnecessary software; choose the packages carefully you will install. Each application has a set of package groups, so if you are going to set up a Web Server, Apache let's say, only install the packages which are a dependency for the Apache server. Ideally, we want to split roles, and each service should have its physical server.

For example, do not install MySQL or Postgres if you don't need them. If you do need a Database engine, install it onto a different and separate physical server.

I am not going to go through network design. Still, a web server should be in a different server and a completely different network segment other than the database server engine, and these two services should communicate only through a hole in the firewall. The right approach for network design is to split it into segments, and each network segment hosting different services, for example, Web servers at the front, applications and database servers in the middle tier and storage at the back-end.

Note: This is just an example, while it is a relatively good example; you should plan your network carefully and position your servers accordingly to your needs and security design.

A slim system should have about 208 packages; if we start installing more than 500 packages, that is becoming far too many already, the system will become bloated. Having an excessive number of packages installed onto the server will have a negative impact on the server's performance, security, and stability. I would suggest reviewing all packages installed and making sure if you need each one of them. You must do that before you put your server to production, once your server is in production; it becomes challenging to guarantee it's security.

Check how many packages installed

```
[root@e-netsec~]# rpm -qa | wc -l
205
```

Analyze all packages

```
[root@e-netsec~]# rpm -qa > /tmp/all_packages
[root@e-netsec~]# cat /tmp/all_packages | more
```

Review each package and research them on the Internet, make sure you know what which one of them is used for, If you don't need it, don't keep it. By reducing the number of software which might have security holes, you are reducing the number of packages which need updating; you are reducing the time the server takes to update all packages.

Don't install X window

The X Windows or graphical environment, it is useful if you are installing a workstation for a regular user. If you are installing a server, there is no need to install the Graphical environment or X Windows. If you are an experienced sysadmin, you will be more productive by using the command line, and you will be making your server much more reliable and secure.

So, don't feel tempted to install it, and if you have installed it, go ahead and remove it. You will feel much happier and won't wake up at night with nightmares.

The command line gives you much more precision, more definition, more accuracy and fast response from your system.

Once you know how to use the command line and have proficiency in using it, you won't stop using it. It is powerful, it gives you more control, and it is excellent.

You won't regret it, remove the X environment and keep your server slim, safer, more reliable and faster. So it is a win/win situation.

Secure your Network TCP/IP stack

Sysctl is an interface used to make changes to the Linux kernel, you can make changes on the fly by typing the command in a shell, and you also can make the changes permanent by editing the file /etc/sysctl.conf and setting the parameter you wish to change.

Sysctl is part of initscripts package it should be on by default Red Hat/Centos systems.

To make your system more secure, we need to make some changes to the TCP/IP stack.

I suggest you add or change the parameters below or simply adjust them.
I am going to give a brief explanation of each one and show how to add them to the /etc/sysctl.conf file.

I strongly advise you to make a backup of all files, prior to any modifications.

```
[root@e-netsec~]# vi /etc/sysctl.conf
```

Note: this is the default configuration file.

```
# Kernel sysctl configuration file for Red Hat Linux
#
# For binary values, 0 is disabled, 1 is enabled.  See sysctl(8) and
# sysctl.conf(5) for more details.
#
# Use '/sbin/sysctl -a' to list all possible parameters.

# Controls IP packet forwarding
net.ipv4.ip_forward = 0

# Controls source route verification
net.ipv4.conf.default.rp_filter = 1

# Do not accept source routing
net.ipv4.conf.default.accept_source_route = 0

# Controls the System Request debugging functionality
of the kernel
kernel.sysrq = 0
```

Note: Since enabling `'SysRq'` gives you physical console access extra abilities, it is recommended to disable it when not troubleshooting a problem or to ensure that physical console access is properly secured.

```
# Controls whether core dumps will append the PID to
the core filename.
# Useful for debugging multi-threaded applications.
kernel.core_uses_pid = 1

# Controls the use of TCP syncookies
net.ipv4.tcp_syncookies = 1

# Controls the default maxmimum size of a mesage queue
kernel.msgmnb = 16384

# Controls the maximum size of a message, in bytes
kernel.msgmax = 65536

# Controls the maximum shared segment size, in bytes
kernel.shmmax = 68719476736

# Controls the maximum number of shared memory
segments, in pages
kernel.shmall = 4294967296
```

We are going to append to the existing file in the following settings:

1. Set `execshield` to protect the kernel and applications from stack and heap overflows
   ```
   kernel.exec-shield=1
   ```

2. Set `kernel.randomize_va_space` to randomize memory segments to make abuse by malicious programs harder.
   ```
   kernel.randomize_va_space=1
   ```

3. Set the `net.ipv4.conf.all.rp_filter` so if a packet is received over an interface and the reverse path is over any other interface the packet will be discarded. Enable IP spoofing protection.
   ```
   net.ipv4.conf.all.rp_filter=1
   ```

4. Set IP source routing, It can allow a user to redirect network traffic for malicious purposes. Therefore, source-based routing should be disabled

   `net.ipv4.conf.all.accept_source_route=0`

5. Set `net.ipv4.icmp_echo_ignore_broadcasts` to Ignore broadcast requests, this way a broadcast ping o sweep ping will not be answered by your server and this way an attacker will have more difficulty finding it.

   `net.ipv4.icmp_echo_ignore_broadcasts=1`

6. Set `net.ipv4.icmp_ignore_bogus_error_messages` controls whether ICMP bogus error message responses are ignored

   `net.ipv4.icmp_ignore_bogus_error_messages=1`

7. Set `net.ipv4.conf.all.log_martians` to make sure spoofed packets get logged.

   `net.ipv4.conf.all.log_martians = 1`

8. Set `net.ipv4.icmp_echo_ignore_all` ignore ICMP request or PING replies:

   `net.ipv4.icmp_echo_ignore_all = 1`

Date and Time

It is crucial to keep your server in sync with time and date. Accurate time is well worth the 'time' and effort. Things like a time stamp on files, log times, Syslog messages, backups, match-up time across devices and troubleshooting problems, including hacking activities, etc.

One way you can keep your Server time in sync is by using an NTP server, make sure you set the server's time correctly to start with, this includes the date.

In RHEL Linux 8, the `ntp` package is deprecated, and the new package is `chrony` (a daemon that runs in user-space).

`chrony` implements an NTP server and an NTP client, which is used to synchronize the system clock with NTP servers, and can be used to synchronize the system clock with a reference clock (e.g a GPS).

It is also used to synchronize the system clock with a manual time input, and as an NTPv4 server or peer to provide a time service to other servers in the network.

Set Date and Time using Command Line

```
[root@e-netsec~]# date --set="20 OCT 2020 16:31"
Tue OCT  20 16:31:00 GMT 2020
```

Configure Chrony

```
[root@e-netsec~]# systemctl start chroyd
```

```
[root@e-netsec~]# systemctl status chroyd
```

```
[root@centossrv01 sysctl.d]# systemctl status chronyd
● chronyd.service - NTP client/server
   Loaded: loaded (/usr/lib/systemd/system/chronyd.service; enabled; vendor preset: enabled)
   Active: active (running) since Sat 2020-10-17 15:55:26 BST; 4 days ago
     Docs: man:chronyd(8)
           man:chrony.conf(5)
 Main PID: 758 (chronyd)
   CGroup: /system.slice/chronyd.service
           └─758 /usr/sbin/chronyd

Oct 17 20:36:06 centossrv01.e-netsec.int chronyd[758]: Selected source 85.119.84.153
Oct 18 04:40:59 centossrv01.e-netsec.int chronyd[758]: Selected source 95.215.175.2
Oct 18 06:21:21 centossrv01.e-netsec.int chronyd[758]: Selected source 85.119.84.153
Oct 18 22:11:46 centossrv01.e-netsec.int chronyd[758]: Selected source 95.215.175.2
Oct 19 02:13:39 centossrv01.e-netsec.int chronyd[758]: Selected source 85.119.84.153
Oct 19 17:05:39 centossrv01.e-netsec.int chronyd[758]: Source 185.53.93.157 replaced with 220.158.215.21
Oct 21 08:41:26 centossrv01.e-netsec.int chronyd[758]: Source 123.50.146.78 replaced with 81.21.76.27
Oct 21 09:50:31 centossrv01.e-netsec.int chronyd[758]: Source 81.21.76.27 replaced with 85.199.214.98
Oct 21 11:29:35 centossrv01.e-netsec.int chronyd[758]: Selected source 85.199.214.98
Oct 21 19:39:51 centossrv01.e-netsec.int chronyd[758]: Source 85.119.84.153 replaced with 81.128.218.110
```

```
[root@e-netsec~]# systemctl enable chroyd
```

Configure Chronyd Server

```
[root@e-netsec~]#  vi /etc/chrony.conf

# Use public servers from the pool.ntp.org project.
# Please consider joining the pool
(http://www.pool.ntp.org/join.html).
server 0.centos.pool.ntp.org iburst
server 1.centos.pool.ntp.org iburst
server 2.centos.pool.ntp.org iburst
server 3.centos.pool.ntp.org iburst

# Record the rate at which the system clock gains/losses time.
driftfile /var/lib/chrony/drift

# Allow the system clock to be stepped in the first three
updates
# if its offset is larger than 1 second.
makestep 1.0 3

# Enable kernel synchronization of the real-time clock (RTC).
rtcsync

# Enable hardware timestamping on all interfaces that support
it.
#hwtimestamp *
```

```
# Increase the minimum number of selectable sources required
to adjust
# the system clock.
#minsources 2
```

Change the Line Below to represent your network

```
# Allow NTP client access from local network.
#allow 192.168.0.0/16
Allow 10.0.0.0/24


# Serve time even if not synchronized to a time source.
#local stratum 10

# Specify file containing keys for NTP authentication.
#keyfile /etc/chrony.keys

# Specify directory for log files.
logdir /var/log/chrony

# Select which information is logged.
#log measurements statistics tracking
```

Restart Chronyd

```
[root@e-netsec~]#  systemctl restart chronyd
```

Add firewall rules

```
[root@e-netsec~]# firewall-cmd –permanent –add-
service=ntp
[root@e-netsec~]# firewall-cmd --reload
```

Configuring the Client

```
[root@e-netsec~]# vi /etc/chrony.conf
# Use public servers from the pool.ntp.org project.
# Please consider joining the pool
(http://www.pool.ntp.org/join.html).
```

Add a line with the IP address for your Chrony Server

```
Server 10.0.0.100
```

```
server 0.centos.pool.ntp.org iburst
server 1.centos.pool.ntp.org iburst
server 2.centos.pool.ntp.org iburst
server 3.centos.pool.ntp.org iburst
```

Restart Chronyd

```
[root@e-netsec~]#  systemctl restart chronyd
```

On the Client check the NTP sources

```
[root@e-netsec~]# chronyc sources
```

On the Server check the NTP Clients

```
[root@e-netsec~]# chronyc clients
```

Applications

Applications reside at the seventh layer of the OSI model; they are the programs we use, the services, which listen for client's connections.
As with all the other aspects of the server, this area is critical, if not the most crucial element of the server to be secured, and probably the most vulnerable layer of them all.

This is also the layer where users interact with the system, and as we all know, we all make mistakes, including developers, by adding BUGs, Security holes, etc.
Systems administrators are also responsible; some choose the easy path and open up the systems by installing unknown packages from unknown sources and by making changes to production servers without testing the results.
For all of these reasons, we must keep a very close eye on this layer.
There are so many useful technologies nowadays to protect a lot of applications; we can use load balancers, application firewalls and many more.

SSH Security

SSH is a protocol (which is also known as Secure Shell); it is a method for secure remote login from one server to another server. It gives many ways for strong authentication; it also protects all communications and integrity with strong encryption. It is a much safer option than protocols (such as telnet, `rlogin,` and FTP) these protocols use clear-text to send and receive data.

While SSH is secure per se, it also needs some attention to make it more secure and keep attackers off your server.

I am going to guide you in keeping your SSH server secure and reliable, by following the steps below:

I strongly advise you to make a backup of all files, before any modifications.

```
[root@e-netsec~]# vi /etc/ssh/sshd_config
```

Set your `/etc/ssh/sshd_config` with parameters similar to the ones below:

```
Port 9977
Version 2
ListenAddress 10.0.0.200
LogLevel INFO
PermitRootLogin NO
MaxAuthTries 3
MaxSessions 3
RhostsRSAAthentication NO
HostbaseAthentication NO
IgnoreRhosts YES
PermitEmptyPasswords NO
Banner /etc/issue.net
AllowUsers user1, user2, user3
ClientAliveInterval 300
ClientAliveCountMax 3
```

Improve further the security of your SSH Server by setting up it to use 2FA (Second Factor Authentication)

There are two very good solutions for 2FA and SSH; they are Google Authenticator (**FREE**) and DUO Security (**Commercial**). I prefer DUO Security because it is easier to set up, it is neat, reliable and very robust.

I am going to show you how to set up your Server to use the *DUO Security* solution for 2FA.

1. Create an account on the DUO Security website

2. Log to the Duo Admin Panel and go to Applications

3. Click Protect an Application and locate UNIX Application in the applications list. Click Protect this Application to get your integration key, secret key, and API hostname.

4. Install pam_duo Prerequisites

   Note: OpenSSL development headers and libraries are required for pam_duo, as well as libpam.

   ```
   [root@e-netsec~]# yum install openssl-devel pam-devel
   ```

5. Install pam_duo
   ```
   [root@e-netsec~]# mkdir /tmp/duo
   [root@e-netsec~]# cd /tmp/duo
   [root@e-netsec~]# wget
   https://dl.duosecurity.com/duo_unix-latest.tar.gz

   [root@e-netsec~]# tar zxf duo_unix-latest.tar.gz

   [root@e-netsec~]#  cd duo_unix-1.11.1
   ```

6. Compile duo_unix

   ```
   [root@e-netsec~]# ./configure --with-pam --prefix=/usr && make && sudo make install
   ```

7. Edit /etc/duo/pam_duo.conf file

   Add Integration Key, Security Key and API hostname

```
[duo]
; Duo integration key
ikey = INTEGRATION_KEY
; Duo secret key
skey = SECRET_KEY
; Duo API hostname        e-NetSec
host = API_HOSTNAME
```

8. PAM **Configuration**

```
[root@e-netsec~]# vi /etc/pam.d/sshd
```

Add the following lines:

```
#%PAM-1.0
auth   required pam_sepermit.so
#auth   include password-auth
auth   required pam_env.so
auth   sufficient pam_duo.so
auth   required pam_deny.so
```

9. Configure /etc/ssh/shd_config

```
[root@e-netsec~]# vi /etc/ssh/shd_config
UsePAM yes
ChallengeResponseAuthentication yes
UseDNS no
```

10.   Edit /etc/pam.d/system-auth

```
[root@e-netsec~]# vi /etc/pam.d/system-auth
```

Add the following lines:

```
auth   required pam_env.so
```

```
# auth   sufficient pam_unix.so nullok try_first_pass
auth   requisite pam_unix.so nullok try_first_pass
auth   sufficient pam_duo.so
auth   requisite pam_succeed_if.so uid >= 500 quiet
auth   required pam_deny.so
```

Update Firewall

```
[root@e-netsec~]# firewall-cmd --permanent --add-
port=2297
[root@e-netsec~]# firewall-cmd --reload
```

Add the following line:

Update /etc/hosts.deny and /etc/hosts.allow

```
[root@e-netsec~]# vi /etc/hosts.deny
```

Add the following line:

```
SSHD:   ALL
```

```
[root@e-netsec~]# vi /etc/hosts.allow
```

Add the following line:

```
SSHD: 172.16.33.0/24
```

You can do so many cool things with SSH, such as; SSH Tunnel, copy a whole system on the fly over the network, and so many more. It is very secure; it encrypts the entire traffic over the network back and forth. It is reliable, and for remote administration, it is excellent. You can run multiple commands at time using cluster, so use more SSH.

If you prefer to use Google Authenticator
Installing Google Authenticator

```
[root@e-netsec~]# yum install
https://dl.fedoraproject.org/pub/epel/epel-release-
latest-7.noarch.rpm

[root@e-netsec~]# yum install google-authenticator -y
```

Once Google Authenticator has been installed, you need to run it. It will ask you few questions and just respond Y to them all.

```
[root@e-netsec~]# google-authenticator
Do you want authentication tokens to be time-based (y/n) y
```

Note: You will see a similar screen on your monitor.

Note: You will need to download the Google Authenticator App to your phone/tablet or similar and scan the QR code to add the account.

```
Do you want me to update your "/root/.google_authenticator"
file? (y/n) y


Do you want to disallow multiple uses of the same
authentication
token? This restricts you to one login about every 30s, but it
increases
your chances to notice or even prevent man-in-the-middle
attacks (y/n) y


By default, a new token is generated every 30 seconds by the
mobile app.
In order to compensate for possible time-skew between the
client and the server,
we allow an extra token before and after the current time.
This allows for a
time skew of up to 30 seconds between authentication server
and client. If you
experience problems with poor time synchronization, you can
increase the window
from its default size of 3 permitted codes (one previous code,
the current
code, the next code) to 17 permitted codes (the 8 previous
codes, the current
code, and the 8 next codes). This will permit for a time skew
of up to 4 minutes
between client and server.
Do you want to do so? (y/n) y


If the computer that you are logging into isn't hardened
against brute-force
login attempts, you can enable rate-limiting for the
authentication module.
By default, this limits attackers to no more than 3 login
attempts every 30s.
Do you want to enable rate-limiting? (y/n) y
```

Configuring SSH with Google Authenticator

```
[root@e-netsec~]# vi /etc/pam.d/sshd
```

Add the following line to the bottom of the file:

```
Auth required pam_google_authenticator.so
[root@e-netsec~]# vi /etc/ssh/sshd_config
```

Change the following line

```
ChallengeResponseAuthentication no
```

To

```
ChallengeResponseAuthentication yes
```

Restart SSH
```
[root@e-netsec~]# systemctml restart sshd.service
```

Test your Server

NOTE: DO NOT USE TELNET OR FTP, THEY ARE CLEAR TEXT, IT IS DANGEROUS!

Web Servers

When talking about web-servers, we most definitively talk about Apache. Apache is the most used web-server on the Internet; it is popular, easy to install and easy to configure. Apache is an excellent choice of a web server.

Apache is a free web server, maintained by the Apache Software Foundation. Apache has been the most popular web server on the Internet since the '90s. Long history and well recorded.

I strongly advise you to make a backup of all files, before any modifications.

Apache on Red Hat/Centos is available and named as 'httpd' package. The main configuration file for Apache can be found at: /etc/httpd/conf/httpd.conf. In this file, you will find most of the parameters you need to configure and make it more secure.
Apache uses a user and group name called apache.

Keep Apache update
```
[root@e-netsec~]# yum update httpd
```

Edit /etc/httpd/conf/httpd.conf file:
```
[root@e-netsec~]# vi /etc/httpd/conf/httpd.conf
```

Disable Trace HTTP Request
```
ServerSignature Off
```

Disable Banner
```
ServerTokens Prod
```

Disable Directory browsing/listing
```
<Directory /var/www/e-netsec.net>
Options -Indexes
</Directory>
```

Restrict Access by IPs or Networks
```
<Directory /var/www/e-netsec.net>
Options -Indexes
AllowOverride None
Order deny,allow
Deny from all
Allow from 192.168.168.0/254
</Directory>
```

Disable Etag
```
FileETag None
```

Disable `AllowOverride` directive

```
<Directory /var/www/e-netsec.net>
Options -Indexes
AllowOverride None
</Directory>
```

Disable Trace

```
TraceEnable off
```

Disable Server Side Include (SSI)

```
<Directory /var/www/e-netsec.net >
Options -Indexes -Includes
Order allow,denyAllow from all
</Directory>
```

Disable unnecessary modules

```
#LoadModule dav_module modules/mod_dav.so
#LoadModule dav_fs_module modules/mod_dav_fs.so
#Include conf/extra/httpd-dav.conf
```

Note: These are just some examples. Analyze your server, check which modules you don't need and disable them.

Limit HTTP Request Methods

```
<LimitExcept GET POST HEAD>
deny from all
</LimitExcept>
```

Access Log

```
LogFormat "%h %l %u %t "\"%{sessionID}C\"
\"%{Referer}i\" \"%{User-Agent}i\" "%r" %>s %b %T"
common
```

Set cookie with secure flag 'HttpOnly'

```
<Directory "/var/www/e-netsec.net ">
    Header set Header edit Set-Cookie ^(.*)$
$1;HttpOnly;Secure
</Directory>
```

Protect against Clickjacking Attack

Add to your .htaccess the following line

```
Header always append X-Frame-Options SAMEORIGIN
```

Protection against Cross Site Scripting (XSS)

Add to your .htaccess the following line

```
<IfModule mod_headers.c>
  Header set X-XSS-Protection "1; mode=block"
</IfModule>
```

Disable HTTP 1.0 Protocol

```
RewriteEngine On
RewriteCond %{THE_REQUEST} !HTTP/1.1$
RewriteRule .* - [F]
```

Disable weak ciphers

Install mod_ssl

```
[root@e-netsec~]# yum install mod_ssl openssl
```

Change folder to:

```
[root@e-netsec~]# cd /etc/httpd/conf.d
```

Edit /etc/httpd/conf.d/ssl.conf file

Replace the following line:

```
SSLCipherSuite
DEFAULT:!EXP:!SSLv2:!DES:!IDEA:!SEED:+3DES
```

With the following line:

```
SSLCipherSuite
ALL:!aNULL:!ADH:!eNULL:!LOW:!EXP:RC4+RSA:+HIGH:+MEDIUM
```

Disable SSL 2.0 and 3.0

```
SSLProtocol all -SSLv2 -SSLv3
```

Enable Stronger Protocol

```
SSLProtocol -ALL +TLSv1.2
```

Tighten folder and file permissions

```
[root@e-netsec~]# chmod -R 750 /etc/httpd/conf
[root@e-netsec~]# chmod -R 750 /etc/httpd/conf.d
```

I also suggest you scan your web server and your application after you modified its configuration to comply with the indicated above. It is crucial to have a baseline of how it looks like from the point security view, assess if any vulnerability found and if any, you need to deal with each before you put your server into production. It is essential to scan your server; it will save you a lot of problems later on.

There are many security scanners, but there are some I recommend, they are free or open-source and easy to install and use.

- http://www.arachni-scanner.com

- https://cirt.net/nikto2/

- https://portswigger.net/burp

FTP Security

FTP is an old protocol that was developed without security in mind. To start with, it is clear-text, which means it sends and receives information in plain text (readable by the world); this is insecure enough in today's computing era.

I suggest you forget about FTP and use SFTP instead, if you cannot use SFTP for whatever reason, I will do my best to write good recommendations to improve its security.

Do not install or use Anonymous FTP if you do not need it!

I strongly advise you to make a backup of all files, before any modifications.

Create a folder to host a certifcate

```
[root@e-netsec~]# mkdir /etc/ssl/vsftp
```

Create the certificate

```
[root@e-netsec~]# openssl req -x509 -nodes -keyout
/etc/ssl/vsftp/vsftpd.pem -out
/etc/ssl/vsftp/vsftpd.pem -days 365 -newkey

rsa:2048

:2048
Generating a 2048 bit RSA private key
........................+++
.................................................+++
writing new private key to '/etc/ssl/vsftp/vsftpd.pem'
-----
You are about to be asked to enter information that will be
incorporated
into your certificate request.
What you are about to enter is what is called a Distinguished Name
or a DN.
There are quite a few fields but you can leave some blank
For some fields, there will be a default value,
If you enter '.', the field will be left blank.
```

```
-----
Country Name (2 letter code) [XX]:GB
State or Province Name (full name) []:Cambridge
Locality Name (eg, city) [Default City]: Cambridgeshire
Organization Name (eg, company) [Default Company Ltd]:e-NetSec Ltd
Organizational Unit Name (eg, section) []:IT
Common Name (eg, your name or your server's hostname) []:web.e-
netsec.net
Email Address []: itsecurity@e-netsec.net
```

All statements for securing your FTP are listed below, edit your configuration file and change it accordingly and make sure you test your server before putting it to production.

Edit /etc/vsftpd/vsftpd.conf file

```
[root@e-netsec~]# vi /etc/vsftpd/vsftpd.conf
```

Settings to Change/add

```
anonymous_enable=NO
anon_upload_enable=NO
anon_mkdir_write_enable=NO
idle_session_timeout=60
data_connection_timeout=90
nopriv_user=ftpsecure
async_abor_enable=NO
ascii_upload_enable=NO
ascii_download_enable=NO
ftpd_banner=Add a security message
chroot_local_user=YES
pam_service_name=vsftpd
userlist_enable=YES
tcp_wrappers=YES
ssl_enable=YES
ssl_tlsv1=YES
ssl_sslv2=NO
ssl_sslv3=NO
allow_anon_ssl=NO
force_local_data_ssl=YES
force_local_logins_ssl=YES
require_ssl_reuse=NO
```

```
chroot_local_user=YES
chroot_list_enable=YES
ssl_ciphers=HIGH
pasv_min_port=40000
pasv_max_port=50000
debug_ssl=YES
```

Restart the FTP server

```
[root@e-netsec~]# systemctl restart vsftpd
```

Open the Necessary Ports on your Firewall

Create rules to allow the following ports:

- 990
- 40000:5000

Add the rules below:

```
[root@e-netsec~]# firewall-cmd --permanent -add-
port=40000:50000/tcp
[root@e-netsec~]# firewall-cmd --permanent -add-
port=990/tcp
```

Allow users to access your FTP server

```
[root@e-netsec~]# vi /etc/vsftpd/chroot_list
```

Add the users allowed to access your FTP Server

```
ftp_userA
ftp_userB
ftp_userC
```

SFTP (mysftp shell)

SFTP is a secure FTP built into SSH (Secure Shell). It is safe because it uses encryption by default. It is slim and doesn't have a lot of software dependencies, and in terms of configuration, it is straightforward and quick to set up. It works straight out of the box, you just need to install the SSH package, and that is it.

Of course, you need to take some steps to secure it even further, but there aren't many things you need to do.

I strongly advise you to make a backup of all files, before any modifications.

Create the SFTP folder

```
[root@e-netsec~]# mkdir -p /data/sftp
```

Set the folder permission

```
[root@e-netsec~]# chmod 701 /data
```

Create Group and User

```
[root@e-netsec~]# groupadd enetsec-sftp
[root@e-netsec~]# useradd -g enetsec-sftp -d /upload -s
/sbin/nologin enetsec-sftp
```

Create User's Folder

```
[root@e-netsec~]# mkdir -p /data/enetsec-sftp/upload
```

Set User/group ownership

```
[root@e-netsec~]# chown -R root:enetsec-sftp
/data/enetsec-sftp
```

```
[root@e-netsec~]# chown -R enetsec-sftp:enetsec-sftp
/data/enetsec-sftp/upload
```

Configure /etc/ssh/sshd_config

```
[root@e-netsec~]# /etc/ssh/sshd_config
```

Add the following lines:

```
Match Group sftpusers
ChrootDirectory /data/%u
ForceCommand e-netsec-sftp
```

Email Security

When we talk about emails, there are two main parts the MTA (Mail Transfer Agent) and MUA (Mail User Agent). The MTA is responsible for delivering mail from one server to another, and the MUA is responsible for delivering emails to users. This is basic! We will be writing about MTA or (Mail Transfer Agent). There are many options available, but I believe Postfix is the best option, it is more secure, it is robust, simple to set up, scalable and it is used by about 30% of Internet servers.

There are multiple MAIL protocols, just to give you a quick list: POP3, SMTP, IMAP, IMAPS etc.

We will cover the SMTP protocol or (Simple Mail Transfer Protocol), this is the protocol used by many servers to transfer emails one to another on the Internet and local Network.

The main SMTP servers for Linux are: Sendmail, Postfix and Qmail

I will cover the MTA side of the mail system and Postfix; we will start by installing it, then we will change the permissions on its configuration files, to make it more secure, then we will configure it. Also, it is crucial to keep your server off blacklists. The configuration below will also help in preventing that as well.

I strongly advise you to make a backup of all files, before any modifications.

Installing Postfix:

```
[root@e-netsec~]# yum install postfix
```

Postfix change permissions:

```
[root@e-netsec~]# chmod 755 /etc/postfix
[root@e-netsec~]# chmod 644 /etc/postfix/*.cf
```

```
[root@e-netsec~]# chmod 755 /etc/postfix/postfix-
script*
[root@e-netsec~]# chmod 755 /var/spool/postfix
[root@e-netsec~]# chown root:root /var/log/mail*
[root@e-netsec~]# chmod 600 /var/log/mail*
```

Configure /etc/postfix/main.cf file:

```
[root@e-netsec~]# vi /etc/postfix/main.cf
```

Change the lines bellow:

```
myhostname = mail.e-netsec.net
inet_interfaces = 192.168.168.210
mynetworks = 10.1.0.0/16, 192.168.168.0/24, 127.0.0.1
myorigin = e-netsec.net
relay_domains = e-netsec.net
smtpd_banner = $myhostname
default_process_limit = 100
smtpd_client_connection_count_limit = 10
smtpd_client_connection_rate_limit = 30
queue_minfree = 20971520
header_size_limit = 51200
message_size_limit = 10485760
smtpd_recipient_limit = 100
smtpd_recipient_overshoot_limit = 101
smtpd_hard_error_limit = 20
smtpd_client_recipient_rate_limit = 110
smtpd_client_connection_rate_limit = 10
smtpd_client_message_rate_limit = 25
default_extra_recipient_limit = 125
duplicate_filter_limit = 125
default_destination_recipient_limit = 125
smtp_destination_recipient_limit =
$default_destination_recipient_limit
```

Update your Firewall and create rules to allow the following port:

- 25

Update Firewall:

```
[root@e-netsec~]# firewall-cmd –permanent –add-port=25/tcp
```

Make use of TLS with Postfix

What is SASL

Postfix uses the variable/parameter "$mynetworks" to control access to it, for example; who can send email utilizing the server. So far there is no other authentication mechanism available, the server only checks the IP address trying to send email belongs to the trusted network "$mynetworks".

If all your users are within the same network/location, then I don't think you will need to use SASL or SSL/TLS. But, on your network, you have mobile users on the road; you will need another mechanism to authenticate them.

SASL (Simple Authentication and Security Layer) gives a good and reliable mechanism to authenticate users using their username and password. I believe the most well-known implementation of SASL is part of the Cyrus SASL library, but dovecot package also brings a SASL implementation.

What about SSL/TLS?

SASL provides a mechanism to authenticate remote users by username and password to relay mail through the server. The issue here is; these mechanisms are sending usernames and passwords in clear-text across the Internet. SASL solves this issue supporting various encrypted authentication methods such as DIGEST-MD5. SSL (Secure Sockets Layer), and more recently TLS (Transport Layer Security) gives a mechanism to encrypt communications between two hosts, in our case our mail server and our remote client. SSL was renamed TLS by the IETF.

Sysadmin

Systems administrators have a critical role in keeping servers secure. They deal with the servers in a daily bases; they keep servers update; they check logs, back them up and know an awful lot about each server, their behaviour, and their problems.

Systems administrators need to have a secure approach and not just do what is easy to make their lives easier; this is the first aspect of security in my opinion; `complacency`.

A lot of Sysadmins are complacent, they install packages which they do not know the precedence, leave servers logged on, and they use simple passwords or even the same passwords for all servers and services. Security starts by changing IT attitude and mentality towards what is security.

Security Policy

Long had gone the days when we did not need to worry about security, and we could trust everyone and anyone on the Internet. The same way it is fundamental for a company to have its corporate network linked to the Internet, it is equally important to have a set of rules or guidelines to protect against the danger which the Internet poses. We see on the TV all the time, and we read everywhere about Cyber Security and breaches, hackers stealing information, vulnerabilities, Zero-Day Attacks, and so many worrying things. It is essential to take some time and think about what is valuable (in terms of data and asset), what needs to be secured. What data needs protection and who can access it, which users are allowed access to the database or the finance server etc.

A security policy is nothing more than some guidelines written on a document, which outline the critical items in a business that needs to be protected. This document will include the company's network, its physical building, server room, assets, data and, etc. The Security Policy also needs to highlight potential threats to all items listed. If the aim of the cybersecurity policy is the threats, we could split it into two categories; those that are coming from the inside (disgruntled employees) which can exfiltrate information, sabotage the company's network or disrupt services. There are also those coming from outside; for example, a hacker could penetrate your defences and cause data loss by modifying it or deleting. There is also physical damage to computers, servers, and network devices.

Once we have identified some or all threats, we need to assess the chances of them happening. As a business, we also need to determine how to prevent or avoid those threats. Training employees is essential and making sure everyone is aware of the security policy and where to find it. The Cyber Security Policy also needs to cover what to do when a threat happens. Last, the Cybersecurity Policy needs to be reviewed and updated regularly, and new employees need a copy.

I would say; It is imperative every one buys into it, from top to bottom, from senior management to admin personnel.

There are plenty of sites which offer templates, which you can use to guide you through this process.

Don't log as root

It amazes me how many systems administrators log in as root to execute simple tasks. We need to use the root account as a last resort. Daily, we need to use ordinary user accounts, and if we do want to run some admin tasks, the best way is to use a tool called 'sudo'.

My advice here is as follows; set a strong password for the root account and don't use it.

You should disable login using the root account altogether, by setting the root account's shell to `/sbin/nologin` in the `/etc/passwd` file or using the `/etc/securetty` file we mentioned in the previous chapter.

I strongly advise you to make a backup of all files, before any modifications.

1. Edit `/etc/passwd`
```
[root@e-netsec~]# vi /etc/passwd
```

Change the line below:

```
root:x:0:0:root:/root:/bin/bash
```

To

```
root:x:0:0:root:/root:/sbin/nologin
```

Enable automatic log out

It is easy to log in as root and forget the console open, to safeguard against these unattended login sessions and reduce this risk, you should configure your server to log out idle users after a fixed period automatically.

Logged as root, add the following lines at the beginning of the `/etc/profile` file to make sure the processing of this file cannot be interrupted:

```
[root@e-netsec~]# vi /etc/profile
trap "" 1 2 3 15
after 120 seconds:
```

```
export TMOUT=60
readonly TMOUT
```

The `TMOUT` variable terminates the shell if there is no activity for the specified number of seconds (set to 60 in the above example).

Disabling root SSH logins

1. Edit `/etc/ssh/sshd_config`, and change the line that reads:

```
[root@e-netsec~]# vi /etc/ssh/sshd_config
```

```
#PermitRootLogin yes
```

To

```
PermitRootLogin no
```

Following all these recommendations, you will be taking serious steps to secure your server and its integrity.

Lock important config files

There is a very nice tool which will do just that! The `Chattr` (Change Attribute) package, is a Linux command utility it can set and unset attributes to files in a Linux File System and keeps essential files and folders, secure from accidental deletion and modifications, even logged as root.

Using `chattr` in a native Linux filesystem, for example; `ext2`, `ext3`, and `ext4`, all flags are supported. Users cannot modify files or folders protected with the attributes set with `chattr` even if you have full permission. See example below:

```
[root@e-netsec~]# chattr +i /etc/inittab.
```

My advice is; check which configuration files are most important to your server and you, change their attributes using `Chattr +i`, then `rename Chattr` command, to a name only you recognize, something different.

We are building yet another layer of protection. Keep adding layers to discourage as many attackers as possible.

LOCK MAC address

Each NIC has a MAC (Media Access Control) address assigned to it; this is a unique number that each NIC (Network Interface Card) has. MAC addresses are 48Bit long and written in HEX Decimal numbers. They work at the Data Link Layer of the OSI Model.

Two things we can do to improve our server security at this layer;

I strongly advise you to make a backup of all files, before any modifications.

1. Configure `udev` and set each NICs MAC address, so they don't change the order at boot time.

   a) `[root@e-netsec~]# vi /etc/udev/rules.d/70-persistent-net.rules`
   Note: you should see something similar to the screenshot below. See where it says: `ATTR{address}=="08:00:27:40:21:5b"`

```
root@localhost:/etc/udev/rules.d
 This file was automatically generated by the /lib/udev/write_net_rules
# program, run by the persistent-net-generator.rules rules file.
#
# You can modify it, as long as you keep each rule on a single
# line, and change only the value of the NAME= key.

# PCI device 0x8086:0x100e (e1000)
SUBSYSTEM=="net", ACTION=="add", DRIVERS=="?*", ATTR{address}=="08:00:27:40:21:5b", ATTR{type}=="1", KERNEL=="eth*", NAME="eth0"
```

e-NetSec

b) Check if this matches the MAC address for your server and each NIC.

c) Edit the file: `/etc/sysconfig/network-scripts/ifcfg-eth0` or `/etc/sysconfig/network-scripts/ifcfg-ens192`

Note: replace `ifcfg-ethX` with the number of your network card.

Note: On RHEL8 the way network cards are named has changed to something like `ifcfg-ens192`

d) Check if the file `/etc/sysconfig/network-scripts/ifcfg-eth0` contain the same MAC address as the one in the `udev` file.

```
[root@localhost network-scripts]# cat ifcfg-eth0
DEVICE=eth0
HWADDR=08:00:27:40:21:5B
TYPE=Ethernet
UUID=4bd8c164-a978-4955-9547-55569a2b14c4
ONBOOT=yes
NM_CONTROLLED=no
BOOTPROTO=dhcp
[root@localhost network-scripts]#
```
e-NetSec

2. Set your switch port to use port-security mac-address, also called sticky MAC.

a) Log to your switch
b) Enable
   Follow the example below:

```
switch# configure terminal
switch(config)# interface ethernet 1/5
```

```
switch(config-if)# switchport port-security mac-
address sticky
switch(config-if)# switchport port-security mac-
address 0050.3e8d.6400
```

Accounts

When you install Linux, some of the packages, they create unnecessary users, while they can have very little harm, I believe that the correct Security Policy we should have in mind is; if we don't need it, don't install it or get rid of it. This principle should also be true for accounts; if you have any disabled users, then it is best to remove these accounts.

I strongly advise you to make a backup of all files, before any modifications.

```
[root@e-netsec~]# vi /etc/passwd

root:x:0:0:root:/root:/bin/bash
bin:x:1:1:bin:/bin:/sbin/nologin
daemon:x:2:2:daemon:/sbin:/sbin/nologin
adm:x:3:4:adm:/var/adm:/sbin/nologin
lp:x:4:7:lp:/var/spool/lpd:/sbin/nologin
sync:x:5:0:sync:/sbin:/bin/sync
shutdown:x:6:0:shutdown:/sbin:/sbin/shutdown
halt:x:7:0:halt:/sbin:/sbin/halt
mail:x:8:12:mail:/var/spool/mail:/sbin/nologin
operator:x:11:0:operator:/root:/sbin/nologin
games:x:12:100:games:/usr/games:/sbin/nologin
ftp:x:14:50:FTP User:/var/ftp:/sbin/nologin
nobody:x:99:99:Nobody:/:/sbin/nologin
systemd-network:x:192:192:systemd Network Management:/:/sbin/nologin
dbus:x:81:81:System message bus:/:/sbin/nologin
polkitd:x:999:998:User for polkitd:/:/sbin/nologin
apache:x:48:48:Apache:/usr/share/httpd:/sbin/nologin
libstoragemgmt:x:998:997:daemon           account           for
libstoragemgmt:/var/run/lsm:/sbin/nologin
abrt:x:173:173::/etc/abrt:/sbin/nologin
rpc:x:32:32:Rpcbind Daemon:/var/lib/rpcbind:/sbin/nologin
```

```
sshd:x:74:74:Privilege-separated SSH:/var/empty/sshd:/sbin/nologin
postfix:x:89:89::/var/spool/postfix:/sbin/nologin
chrony:x:997:995::/var/lib/chrony:/sbin/nologin
ntp:x:38:38::/etc/ntp:/sbin/nologin
tcpdump:x:72:72::/:/sbin/nologin
renato:x:1000:1000:renato:/home/renato:/bin/bash
```

This is the default `/etc/passwd` file which comes with Red Hat/Centos. Straightaway we can see a few candidates for being deleted, such as:

- `lp` (if you don't have a printer, get rid of it!)
- `uucp` (if you don't run `uucp` service, get rid of it)
- `games` (if it is a server, do you need this account?)
- `gopher` (I doubt you have this service, get rid of it)
- `ftp` (if you don't run an FTP server, get rid of it)

Note: We understand these accounts have very little to offer in securing your system, as some of them use the SHELL as `/sbin/nologin`, but having fewer accounts on your system also reduces the surface and unnecessary worries. If you don't need some of these accounts, get rid of it!

Burry the root password

In the sysadmin world, `sudo` is a vital tool! It allows users to do their admin tasks without giving root access.

Sudo is simple to use, simple to configure and simple to manage; it is a dream for sysadmin fighting against the desire of 'wannabe' root users.

The `sudo` command allows you to run programs with the security privileges of the `superuser`, root. It will require you to type in your password and confirms if you are allowed to execute the command requested by checking the `sudoers` file, which we configure in advance. By configuring the `sudoers` file, your sysadmin can give specific users or groups access to some or all commands without giving root access to the server. All commands typed at the shell are logged and recorded.

I strongly advise you to make a backup of all files, before any modifications.

Configure /etc/sudoers file

```
[root@e-netsec~]# visudo

## Allow root to run any commands anywhere
renato  ALL=(ALL)        ALL
```

The configuration above gives the user 'renato' full root privileges, without the root password.

Using Sudo

```
[renato@e-netsec~]# sudo /usr/sbin/ip a
```

We trust you have received the usual lecture from the local System

Administrator. It usually boils down to these three things:

```
    #1) Respect the privacy of others.
    #2) Think before you type.
    #3) With great power comes great responsibility.

[sudo] password for renato:
eth0      Link encap:Ethernet  HWaddr 08:00:27:40:21:5B
          inet addr:10.0.0.30  Bcast:10.0.0.255
Mask:255.255.255.0
          inet6 addr: fe80::a00:27ff:fe40:215b/64
Scope:Link
```

```
         UP BROADCAST RUNNING MULTICAST  MTU:1500
Metric:1
         RX packets:783665 errors:0 dropped:0
overruns:0 frame:0
         TX packets:84373 errors:0 dropped:0
overruns:0 carrier:0
         collisions:0 txqueuelen:1000
         RX bytes:79757149 (76.0 MiB)  TX
bytes:16015286 (15.2 MiB)

lo        Link encap:Local Loopback
          inet addr:127.0.0.1  Mask:255.0.0.0
          inet6 addr: ::1/128 Scope:Host
          UP LOOPBACK RUNNING  MTU:65536  Metric:1
          RX packets:66 errors:0 dropped:0 overruns:0
frame:0
          TX packets:66 errors:0 dropped:0 overruns:0
carrier:0
          collisions:0 txqueuelen:0
          RX bytes:7834 (7.6 KiB)  TX bytes:7834 (7.6
KiB)
```

Host-Based Intrusion Detection System

No system will be secure without a HIDS (Host-based Intrusion Detection System). An Intrusion Detection System can monitor and analyze a computing system and its layers going through the network packets processed by the network interface card and applications.

A Host-based (Intrusion Detection System) analyses traffic to and from specific hosts, where the intrusion detection mechanism is installed and configured. It can monitor essential system files and attempt to modify such files, for example; /etc/passwd, etc.

I believe a Host-based Intrusion Detection System needs to be on any host connected directly to the Internet or not. Many attacks come from internal threats. Knowing which services/applications are trying to modify or even modify the configuration files is very important.

There are many options on the market, but the one I like, use, and recommend is OSSEC. OSSEC is free (open source), easy to install, to configure, and manage. OSSEC scales well and can install onto many OSs (Linux, OpenBSD, Solaris, and Windows). It has a good engine for correlation and analysis, log analysis, file integrity checking, Windows registry monitoring, centralized policy enforcement, rootkit detection, real-time alerting, and active response.

https://www.ossec.net/

The commercial option which I like and have used is TripWire. It is good, but it is not free.

https://www.tripwire.com/products/tripwire-enterprise/

Some Important OSSEC Features

- Real-time and Configurable Alerts
- Centralized management
- Agent and agentless monitoring
- Log Monitoring
- Rootkit detection
- Active response

OSSEC Installation

1. Create a folder to download and compile OSSEC

```
[renato@e-netsec~]# mkdir /usr/local/src/ossec
[renato@e-netsec~]# cd /usr/local/src/ossec
```

2. Download OSSEC

```
[renato@e-netsec~]# wget https://github.com/ossec/ossec-
hids/archive/3.6.0.tar.gz
```

3. Uncompress OSSEC

```
[renato@e-netsec~]# tar -zxvf 3.6.0.tar.gz
[renato@e-netsec~]# cd /usr/local/ossec/ossec-hids-3.6.0
```

4. Install OSSEC

```
[renato@e-netsec~]# ./install.sh
```

Note: The installation script will ask some questions to answer them to get it up and running. We need to choose if we are installing a server or agent.

** For installation in English, choose [en].

OSSEC HIDS v3.6.0 Installation Script - http://www.ossec.net

You are about to start the installation process of the OSSEC HIDS. You must have a C compiler pre-installed in your system.

 - System: Linux centos8.e-netsec.int 4.18.0-193.el8.x86_64
 - User: root
 - Host: centos8.e-netsec.int

-- Press ENTER to continue or Ctrl-C to abort. --

 - Server installation chosen.

2- Setting up the installation environment.

 - Choose where to install the OSSEC HIDS [/var/ossec]:

3- Configuring the OSSEC HIDS.

3.1- Do you want e-mail notification? (y/n) [y]:
    3.1- Do you want e-mail notification? (y/n) [y]: y

- What's your e-mail address? info@e-netsec.net
- What's your SMTP server ip/host? mx.e-netsec.net
3.2- Do you want to run the integrity check daemon? (y/n) [y]:
- Running syscheck (integrity check daemon).

3.3- Do you want to run the rootkit detection engine? (y/n) [y]:
- Running rootcheck (rootkit detection).

3.4- Active response allows you to execute a specific
command based on the events received. For example,
you can block an IP address or disable access for
a specific user.
More information at:
http://www.ossec.net/en/manual.html#active-response

- Do you want to enable active response? (y/n) [y]:
- Active response enabled.

- By default, we can enable the host-deny and the
firewall-drop responses. The first one will add
a host to the /etc/hosts.deny and the second one
will block the host on iptables (if linux) or on
ipfilter (if Solaris, FreeBSD or NetBSD).
- They can be used to stop SSHD brute force scans,
portscans and some other forms of attacks. You can
also add them to block on snort events, for example.

- Do you want to enable the firewall-drop response? (y/n) [y]:
- firewall-drop enabled (local) for levels >= 6

- 10.0.0.1

- Do you want to add more IPs to the white list? (y/n)? [n]:
3.5- Do you want to enable remote syslog (port 514 udp)? (y/n) [y]:
- Remote syslog enabled.

3.6- Setting the configuration to analyze the following logs:

- If you want to monitor any other file, just change

the ossec.conf and add a new localfile entry.
Any questions about the configuration can be answered
by visiting us online at http://www.ossec.net .

   --- Press ENTER to continue ---

- System is Redhat Linux.
  - Init script modified to start OSSEC HIDS during boot.

 - Configuration finished properly.

 - To start OSSEC HIDS:
     /var/ossec/bin/ossec-control start

 - To stop OSSEC HIDS:
     /var/ossec/bin/ossec-control stop

   -   The   configuration   can   be   viewed   or   modified   at
/var/ossec/etc/ossec.conf

   Thanks for using the OSSEC HIDS.
   If you have any question, suggestion or if you find any bug,
   contact us at https://github.com/ossec/ossec-hids or using
   our public maillist at
   https://groups.google.com/forum/#!forum/ossec-list

   More information can be found at http://www.ossec.net

   --- Press ENTER to finish (maybe more information below). ---

 - In order to connect agent and server, you need to add each agent
to the server.
   Run the 'manage_agents' to add or remove them:

   /var/ossec/bin/manage_agents

   More information at:

Note: OSSEC will need the following dvel packages in order to be successfully compiled:

- make.x86_64
- gcc.x86_64
- pcre2-devel.x86_64
- pcre.x86_64
- sendmail-milter.x86_64
- sendmail-milter-devel.x86_64
- libevent.x86_64
- libevent-devel.x86_64
- zlib.x86_64
- zlib-devel.x86_64
- openssl.x86_64
- openssl-libs.x86_64
- openssl-devel.x86_64

Start OSSEC Service

```
[renato@e-netsec~]#        /var/ossec/bin/ossec-control
start
```

Set OSSEC as an agent or server
```
[renato@e-netsec~]# /var/ossec/bin/manage_agents
```

Check OSSEC log
```
[renato@e-netsec~]# tail -50 /var/ossec/logs/ossec.log
```

Get Rid of Offenders

OSSEC will block attacks at any time; many times, an attacker will try multiple times, even a million times, and eventually, he/she will succeed. OSSEC has excellent features, and one of them helps with this problem, and keeps a record of offending IPs and blocks them for a more extended period. This feature is known as "Repeated Offenders."

This feature allows you to specify how long an IP address will be banned for in minutes, and it will increase the duration as the attack go on.

Note: This feature is not on by default.

I strongly advise you to make a backup of all files before any modifications.

Edit /var/ossec/etc/ossec.conf

Search for the "Active Response" section, and between the tags, add the following:

```
<active-response>
  <repeated_offenders>30,60,120</repeated_offenders>
</active-response>
```

Check Integrity with AIDE

Advanced Intrusion Detection Environment (AIDE) this is a great utility that creates a database of files on the system, and uses the database to make sure files have their integrity.

Installing AIDE

```
[renato@e-netsec~]# yum search aide

[renato@e-netsec~]# yum install aide.x86_64
```

Generate Databse
```
[renato@e-netsec~]# aide -init
Start timestamp: 2020-10-26 14:24:40 +0000 (AIDE 0.16)
AIDE initialized database at /var/lib/aide/aide.db.new.gz

Number of entries:       69014


--------------------------------------------------
The attributes of the (uncompressed) database(s):
--------------------------------------------------
```

```
/var/lib/aide/aide.db.new.gz
   MD5        : 0Ar0TqVP7p/7JKqYAe87dA==
   SHA1       : MO1BMBDIBoWsDw6393U23l8ize4=
   RMD160     : noGX/mK66vv6y/y+B+gPFJeGRuw=
   TIGER      : r4nsfCNFlr7LyimySgAe6aizlmv02Qmo
   SHA256     : JEVE8ztopjIKEVBuFPZlonYelZ8qPW9A
                oM7BkIF1koY=
   SHA512     : wEM24CGMsKD14ZUFde6unZdRiOZSWZGQ
                LFVT8/z1AFxFYVisUQYlba3FpBv00ZLW
                fnyCYNHPcT3z6w5R0s9+jg==
End timestamp: 2020-10-26 14:25:47 +0000 (run time: 1m 7s)
```

Start using the databse

```
[root@e-netsec~]# mv /var/lib/aide/aide.db.new.gz
/var/lib/aide/aide.db.gz
```

Running a check

```
[root@e-netsec~]# aide --check
Start timestamp: 2020-10-26 14:32:44 +0000 (AIDE 0.16)
AIDE  found  NO  differences  between  database  and  filesystem.
Looks okay!!

Number of entries:         69014


---------------------------------------------------
The attributes of the (uncompressed) database(s):
---------------------------------------------------

/var/lib/aide/aide.db.gz
   MD5        : 0Ar0TqVP7p/7JKqYAe87dA==
   SHA1       : MO1BMBDIBoWsDw6393U23l8ize4=
   RMD160     : noGX/mK66vv6y/y+B+gPFJeGRuw=
   TIGER      : r4nsfCNFlr7LyimySgAe6aizlmv02Qmo
   SHA256     : JEVE8ztopjIKEVBuFPZlonYelZ8qPW9A
                oM7BkIF1koY=
   SHA512     : wEM24CGMsKD14ZUFde6unZdRiOZSWZGQ
                LFVT8/z1AFxFYVisUQYlba3FpBv00ZLW
                fnyCYNHPcT3z6w5R0s9+jg==
```

End timestamp: 2020-10-26 14:33:49 +0000 (run time: 1m 5s)

Automating System checks

```
[root@e-netsec~]# crontab -e
05 4 * * * root /usr/sbin/aide --check
```

Audating AIDE's database

```
[root@e-netsec~]# aide --update
```

Fail2ban

Fail2ban is a security tool that scans log files, for example, /var/log/apache/error_log, and bans the IPs not behaving well, IPs with many password failures, too many connections from the same IPs, etc. Fail2Ban works by updating iptables rules to reject the misbehaving IPs for a specified amount of time. The default configuration for Fail2Ban comes with filters for various services, such as; apache, ssh, etc

Fail2Ban can help to reduce the number of incorrect authentication attempts, but it cannot eliminate the risk; to eliminate such a risk, we need to use a Second Factor Authentication (2FA) mechanism.

I strongly advise you to make a backup of all files before any modifications.

Installing Fail2Ban

To install fail2ban we need to install Epel repo. I have been using Epel for some time now, and I believe it is relatively safe.

Install Epel Repo

```
[root@e-netsec~]# yum search epel-release.noarch
[root@e-netsec~]# yum install epel-release.noarch
```

Install fail2ban

```
[root@e-netsec~]# yum install fail2ban.noarch
```

Configuring fail2ban

Make a copy of `/etc/fail2ban/jail.conf`

```
[root@e-netsec~]#
cp /etc/fail2ban/jail.conf /etc/fail2ban/jail.local
```

Note: this step is necessary because you should not edit the `jail.conf` file directly.

Edit `/etc/fail2ban/jail.local` file

```
[root@e-netsec~]# vi /etc/fail2ban/jail.local
```

Configure the SSH Section

```
[ssh-iptables]
enabled = true
filter = sshd
action = iptables[name=SSH, port=ssh, protocol=tcp]
sendmail-whois[name=SSH, dest=sysadmin@e-netsec.net,
sender=fail2ban@e-netsec.net]
logpath = /var/log/auth.log
maxretry = 5
logpath=/var/log/secure
```

Configure Postfix Section

```
[postfix-tcpwrappers]
enabled = true
filter = postfix
action = hostsdeny
sendmail[name=Postfix, dest=sysadmin@e-netsec.net]
logpath = /var/log/maillog
```

```
maxretry = 3
bantime = 800
findtime = 800
```

Note: You can also configure fail2ban to protect Apache against those annoying IPs which fill in the access log and many other applications. Take at fail2ban documentation.

SELinux (Security-Enhanced Linux)

The SELinux (Security-Enhanced Linux) brings another layer of security for your server; it gives more granular control over objects. It was originally developed by the NSA (National Security Agency) and Red Hat. It comes by default installed in most Linux distributions based on the RPM system (Red Hat and Centos), for example.

This is such a great security layer for servers facing the Public Internet.

There are two main modes of access control
  a) DAC (Discretionary Access Control)
  b) MAC (Mandatory Access control)

DAC is what we know as file permissions, and these permissions are set at the discretion of the sysadmins, and it is prone to breaches by Malware and exploits. Accesses to files are allowed by looking at the UID and GID.

MAC, on the other hand, is more granular and has two main divisions or classes; subject (user/process) and object (files in general); this is the type of security layer which is offered by SELinux, whereby sysadmins have more control over objects. It does require more knowledge than DAC, but once you have mastered it, it will become easy to implement, very flexible, and powerful.

SELinux is normally compiled into the kernel of most rpm distribution, such as; Red Hat/Centos. It allows one to label objects and subjects, and it does not allow interaction between subjects and objects by default. This is enforced by the creation of 'domains' to group subjects. These domains are also compared to 'sandboxes.' For example, one can create a domain name called 'frontend' and group all files from the `httpd` package.

SELinux has mainly three mores:
  a) `Enforcing`
  b) `Permissive`

c) Disabled

To enable SELinux is very easy and quick. You can enable/disable in a few different ways, such as:

1. You can pass arguments to the kernel at boot time to enable it
2. You can edit the file `/etc/sysconfig/selinux`
   Note: this is actually a symbolic link to `../selinux/config`.

Check if SELinux was compiled into the kernel

```
[root@e-netsec~]# cd /boot

[root@e-netsec~]# cat config-3.10.0-1127.el7.x86_64 |
grep -i seli
CONFIG_SECURITY_SELINUX=y
CONFIG_SECURITY_SELINUX_BOOTPARAM=y
CONFIG_SECURITY_SELINUX_BOOTPARAM_VALUE=1
CONFIG_SECURITY_SELINUX_DISABLE=y
CONFIG_SECURITY_SELINUX_DEVELOP=y
CONFIG_SECURITY_SELINUX_AVC_STATS=y
CONFIG_SECURITY_SELINUX_CHECKREQPROT_VALUE=1
# CONFIG_SECURITY_SELINUX_POLICYDB_VERSION_MAX is not set
CONFIG_DEFAULT_SECURITY_SELINUX=y
CONFIG_DEFAULT_SECURITY="selinux"
```

Enable SELinux

You can also turn SElinux ON and OFF by just, make sure ythe line SELINUX=enforcing

```
[root@e-netsec~]# vi /etc/sysconfig/selinux

# This file controls the state of SELinux on the
system.
# SELINUX= can take one of these three values:
#      enforcing - SELinux security policy is enforced.
#      permissive - SELinux prints warnings instead of
enforcing.
#      disabled - No SELinux policy is loaded.
```

111

```
SELINUX=enforcing
# SELINUXTYPE= can take one of these two values:
#       targeted - Targeted processes are protected,
#       mls - Multi Level Security protection.
SELINUXTYPE=targeted
```

Check SELinux status

```
[root@e-netsec~]# sestatus -v
SELinux status:                 enabled
SELinuxfs mount:                /selinux
Current mode:                   enforcing
Mode from config file:          enforcing
Policy version:                 24
Policy from config file:        targeted

Process contexts:
Current context:
unconfined_u:unconfined_r:unconfined_t:s0-s0:c0.c1023
Init context:                   system_u:system_r:init_t:s0
/sbin/mingetty                  system_u:system_r:getty_t:s0
/usr/sbin/sshd                  system_u:system_r:sshd_t:s0-
s0:c0.c1023

File contexts:
Controlling term:
unconfined_u:object_r:user_devpts_t:s0
/etc/passwd                     system_u:object_r:etc_t:s0
/etc/shadow                     system_u:object_r:shadow_t:s0
/bin/bash                       system_u:object_r:shell_exec_t:s0
/bin/login                      system_u:object_r:login_exec_t:s0
/bin/sh                         system_u:object_r:bin_t:s0 ->
system_u:object_r:shell_exec_t:s0
/sbin/agetty                    system_u:object_r:getty_exec_t:s0
/sbin/init                      system_u:object_r:init_exec_t:s0
/sbin/mingetty                  system_u:object_r:getty_exec_t:s0
/usr/sbin/sshd                  system_u:object_r:sshd_exec_t:s0
```

A lot of sysadmins disable SELinux, because it is easy to ignore it, then trying to use it and make it work. I agree; it is more comfortable, but not secure.

Red Hat and Centos comes with some default policies, which we can start using it and add to it to increase the server's security.

SELinux separates subjects from objects using labels. The labels refer to security context: `user:role:type`

To see the security labels of a file:
```
[root@e-netsec~]# ls -sZ
-rw-------. root root system_u:object_r:admin_home_t:s0 anaconda-
ks.cfg
-rw-r--r--. root root unconfined_u:object_r:admin_home_t:s0 bl
-rw-r--r--. root root system_u:object_r:admin_home_t:s0 install.log
-rw-r--r--. root root system_u:object_r:admin_home_t:s0
install.log.syslog
```

In order to enforce some security rules to a group of files, we need to label them as part of the same domain. Files that are not labelled will not be protected by SELinux. To make sure you label all files non-labelled, all you need to do is creating a file at the root filesystem `/.autorelabel`. This will relabel all files after your server has been rebooted.

You can also use the command `fixfiles`, and this will also relabel all files throughout the whole filesystem.

A good example I like using; you have an Apache web server, and you change the `DocumentRoot` folder to a different volume. If you don't make the correct changes to the new `DocumentRoot` folder, Apache won't have the permissions to server the pages. This will break your applications.

1. Create a folder to become the new `DocumentRoot`
```
[root@e-netsec~]# mkdir /var/html
```

2. Check the SELinux permissions
```
[root@e-netsec~]# ls -lZ
drwxr-xr-x. root root system_u:object_r:acct_data_t:s0 account
drwxr-xr-x. root root system_u:object_r:var_t:s0       cache
drwxr-xr-x. root root system_u:object_r:var_t:s0       db
drwxr-xr-x. root root system_u:object_r:var_t:s0       empty
```

```
drwxr-xr-x. root root  system_u:object_r:public_content_t:s0 ftp
drwxr-xr-x. root root  system_u:object_r:games_data_t:s0 games
drwxr-xr-x. root root  unconfined_u:object_r:var_t:s0    html
```

3. Create an index.html

```
[root@e-netsec~]# touch /var/html/index.html
[root@e-netsec~]# echo "Welcome to e-netsec" >
/var/html/index.html
```

4. **Edit** `/etc/httpd/conf/httpd.conf` change the `DocumentRoot` path

```
[root@e-netsec~]# vi /etc/httpd/conf/httpd.conf

#DocumentRoot "/var/www/html"

DocumentRoot /var/html
```

5. Restart Apache

```
[root@e-netsec~]# systemctl restart restart
```

6. Open your browser and navigate to your Server's IP http://10.0.0.30

Forbidden

You don't have permission to access / on this server.

Apache/2.2.15 (CentOS) Server at 10.0.0.30 Port 80

Note: This is because the new folder and index.html files (objects) are part of different 'Domain'

```
[root@e-netsec~]# ls -lZ
```

drwxr-xr-x. root root unconfined_u:object_r:var_t:s0   html

drwxr-xr-x. root root system_u:object_r:httpd_sys_content_t:s0 www

Note: They have different Security context.

We can fix that very easily, with a simple command as per below:

Fix objects with different Domains

114

1.
```
[root@e-netsec~]# cd /var
[root@e-netsec~]# chcon -R -t httpd_sys_content_t
html/
```
2. Test your page again,

Welcome Herey

Magically it Works!

As you can see, SELinux is easy, and it will give your server a completely different level of security, one which cannot be by-passed escalating privileges, for example.

Keep your system updated

It is crucial to keep your system or your servers updated. This will help in reducing or eliminating BUGs, security holes such as; Zero-Day Exploit, and many more.

By updating your system frequently, you are already fighting against many attacks out there; you are helping in protecting your systems and the entire Internet. You don't want your server to become a zombie and be controlled remotely to attack other systems on the Internet. You also don't want your server to be blacklisted or have your services disrupted and your hard work to sink.

You can automate these updates and make them happen on a weekly basis or daily basis; the important thing here is; to update your servers frequently.

Automate Updates

Install `yum-cron`

```
yum -y install yum-cron
```

Edit /etc/sysconfig/yum-cron file

```
[root@e-netsec~]# vi /etc/sysconfig/yum-cron


# by default MAILTO is unset, so crond mails the output
by itself
# example:  MAILTO=root
MAILTO= sysadmin@e-netsec.net

# you may set SYSTEMNAME if you want your yum emails
tagged differently
# default is the output of hostname command
# this variable is used only if MAILTO is set too
SYSTEMNAME="mysever.e-netsec.net"

# you may set DAYS_OF_WEEK to the days of the week you
want to run
# default is every day
DAYS_OF_WEEK="6"

# which day should it do a cleanup on? Defaults to 0
(Sunday).  If this day isn't in the
# DAYS_OF_WEEK above, it'll never happen
CLEANDAY="0"
# Disable kernel from being updated
YUM_PARAMETER="-x kernel* "
```

Set the service to start-up boot time

```
[root@e-netsec~]# systemctl enable yum-cron
```

Backups

Backup a server or system is critical. It is one of the most important tasks a Sysadmin can carry. It is a big responsibility to be responsible for your server/system backup.

I am not going to discuss different methods of backing up or talk about specific programs. There is plenty of Backup software on the market, some are open source, and some are commercial, some are good and have useful features, and some are just ok. The message here is to backup your server, if possible hourly, if not daily. Fully backup your server if you can, otherwise choose with care which areas need backing up. Some examples are:

- /etc (all your configuration files)
- /home (if it is a shared system, with multiple users)
- /var (contains all logs for your server)
- /boot (if you compiled a new kernel or modified grub.conf)

These are just some examples; you need to understand your server and the application it is hosting to make sure you are backing up the correct folders. The easiest way is to back up your server fully, but space might be a problem; if it is, choose which folders, and make a daily backup, compare each backup and file backed up to the previous.

Backing up is essential, but treating your back up with care is also essential. Some recommendations:

a) Backup your system/server to a local storage
b) Encrypt it
c) Make an off-site copy of your backup
d) Make sure only authorized people can handle your backup

You will be happy if the day comes when you need to restore your system, and have it fully backed up and up to date.

I would like to point out, there are some technologies which cause some confusion, and they are:

- `Mirroring`
- `Snapshotting`

These two technologies can help recover data quickly, but they are no substitute for the old backup.

Subscribe to Security Alerts

Sign up to security lists, security bulletins, Vulnerability Databases, security alerts, and advisories.
This way, you will be alert and know about most vulnerabilities as soon as they have been discovered.

To be on top of all the security news, and knowing the latest security trends, staying aware of changing threat information is very difficult and time-consuming.

Signing up for such security updates will help keep your system up-to-date and prevent it from being open to vulnerabilities and exploits.

There are many lists, in the US, in the UK, in Europe, but the ones I recommend signing up or keep an eye on them are:

- https://www.kb.cert.org/vuls/
- https://nvd.nist.gov/
- https://www.us-cert.gov/
- https://isc.sans.edu/
- https://www.exploit-db.com/
- https://www.ncsc.gov.uk/index/alerts-and-advisories
- https://www.cisecurity.org/resources/advisory/
- https://www.rapid7.com/db

Monitoring your Server

After this hard work of making your server secure, we need to monitor it. Not just check if it is up or down, but there are many aspects which need to take into account.

Storage, for example, you can suffer from a denial of service by filling up your disks, so it is important to monitor if your disk is not filling up too quickly and be alerted if it is so.

Monitor if your disk all of a sudden is freeing up space too quickly; it could be your data is being deleted. So, monitor all your disks, volumes and partitions.

Monitoring your server's CPU, Memory, and the Load, how many TCP connections it is processing per minute, or if your application is running, if the TCP/UPD ports are listening and active, etc.

I would suggest making a list of all the servers' components and grouping them;

Hardware: Storage (disks/partitions), Memory (RAM/Swapping), CPU, NIC, Power Supply, etc

Operating System: Load (high/low), TCP/UDP connections (Min/Max), UPTIME, Services running (UP/Down), packages (installed/removed), ports (open/closed), logs (created/deleted), Ports ope/closed, Space usage (growing too fast/going down too fast) etc

Applications: Application Status, Application response, Speed, memory usage, etc.

This is just to give you a basic idea, each case is different, but can be used as a starting point.

Shell Commands

Send all commands typed at the shell to a remote Syslog server. You need to cross all Ts and dot all Is. You need to record each, and every command typed in your server's Shell. This data is very important for you to analyze events; let's say you had an issue at 5:00 pm on a given day; by logging all commands daily, you can troll your Syslog Server to the specific date and time and see which commands have been executed. This will give you a very good idea of how the problem began, and also, if there are commands which you do not expect to be executed at the SHELL, you can also have your Syslog to alert for those.

I will show you how to set up your system to capture all commands typed in the shell and send them to a remote Syslog server.

I strongly advise you to make a backup of all files before any modifications.

1. Edit /etc/bashrc
```
[root@e-netsec~]# vi /etc/bashrc
```

Append to the file, the following line:

```
export PROMPT_COMMAND='RETRN_VAL=$?;logger -p
local6.debug "$(whoami) [$$]: $(history 1 | sed "s/^[
]*[0-9]\+[ ]*//" ) [$RETRN_VAL]"'
```

2. Create the following file:
```
[root@e-netsec~]# vi /etc/rsyslog.d/bash.conf
```

Add the following line:

```
local6.*     /var/log/commands.log
```

3. Restart `rsyslog` service

```
[root@e-netsec~]# service rsyslog restart
```

120

Rotate your logs

Log files are a very important piece of data that every server or device generates, and some servers or some devices generate a lot of logs. These logs contain important information about many aspects of the server, such as; hardware information, email info, web server access, and much more.

It is important to rotate these logs frequently. How frequent depends on the number of logs your server generates. For some servers, weekly is fine; for other servers, daily is not. I recommend rotation at least daily, but it all depends on how much your logs grow; if they grow too much hourly, then you would need to rotate them hourly, as simple as this.

Logrotate (`/etc/logrotate.conf`) is a utility that does what it is on the tin; it rotates logs, and it does it in a very simple and easy way. It was written to make the administration of servers that generate a lot of logs. It makes it easier to automate rotation, compression, removal and gives the option to mailing log files. One can set the log files to be rotated daily, weekly, monthly, or when it grows too large.

To configure `logrotate` you need to edit the file `logrotate.conf`, which can be found in `/etc`. I am going to show you how to set it up.

I strongly advise you to make a backup of all files before any modifications.

```
[root@e-netsec~]# vi /etc/logrotate.conf

# see "man logrotate" for details
# rotate log files weekly
weekly

# keep 4 weeks worth of backlogs
rotate 4
```

```
# create new (empty) log files after rotating old ones
create

# use date as a suffix of the rotated file
dateext

# uncomment this if you want your log files compressed
#compress

# RPM packages drop log rotation information into this
directory
include /etc/logrotate.d

# no packages own wtmp and btmp -- we'll rotate them
here
/var/log/wtmp {
    monthly
    create 0664 root utmp
        minsize 1M
    rotate 1
}
```

See the example above; this is the default configuration that comes out of the box with Centos 8. If we need to modify it and change the following parameters:

1. weekly to daily
2. rotate 4 to rotate 1
3. Uncomment #compress

Let's suppose we would like to rotate /var/log/messages; all we need to do is add another section below /var/log/wtmp, like the one below:

```
# Rotate Messages log

/var/log/messages {

    rotate 1

    daily
```

```
    postrotate

        /usr/bin/killall -HUP syslogd

    endscript

}
```

Let's suppose you also want to rotate Apache logs, you do the same as above, add the whole statement below the one for `/var/log/messages`, and see the example:

Rotate Apache's log

```
"/var/log/httpd/access.log" /var/log/httpd/error.log {
    rotate 1
    mail www@e-netsec.net
    size 100k
    sharedscripts
    postrotate
        /usr/bin/killall -HUP httpd
    endscript
}
```

Audit Log

Logs are a very important source of how health your server is, what has happened, and what is happening to it. Check your logs daily or hourly if possible, but check your logs.

They can show you information about many events in your server, such as successful logins, unsuccessful logins, failed attempts, pam modules, and more. In terms of security, all logs are important, but `/var/log/audit/audit`.log is very important, if not the most important on your system, it contains useful information. You should pay particular attention to it and make sure it is rotated accordingly, backed up and, most important, have a mechanism to parse it and extract all necessary information to alert you in case of a breach of security policy or attempt to breach it. The audit log is controlled by the `auditd` process

The list below gives you a summary of the information that Audit is capable of recording in its log files:

- Date, time, type, and outcome of an event.
- Sensitivity labels of subjects and objects.
- Association of an event with the identity of the user who triggered the event.
- All modifications to Audit configuration and attempts to access Audit log files.
- All uses of authentication mechanisms, such as SSH, Kerberos, and others.
- Changes to any trusted database, such as `/etc/passwd`.
- Attempts to import or export information into or from the system.

The audit package comes installed by default on Red Hat and Centos systems, but to install it, it is straightforward.

```
[root@e-netsec~]# yum install audit
```

There are two ways of adding rules, at the command line and by editing the file `/etc/audit/audit.rules`

Let's define a rule that logs all write access to, and every attribute change of, the `/etc/passwd` file,

Run the following command:

```
[root@e-netsec~]# auditctl -w /etc/passwd -p wa -k passwd_changes
```

To make the same rule persistent, all you need it to edit the file `/etc/audit/audit.rules`

```
[root@e-netsec~]# vi /etc/audit/audit.rules
```

Append the following line to the bottom of the file:

```
-w /etc/passwd -p wa -k passwd_changes
```

To see which rules are enabled, run the following command:

```
[root@e-netsec~]# auditctl -l
```
-w /etc/passwd -p wa -k passwd_changes
-w /etc/selinux/ -p wa -k selinux_changes
-w /sbin/insmod -p x -k module_insertion
-a always,exit -F arch=b64 -S adjtimex,settimeofday -F key=time_change

To see a report produced by the audit system, run the following command:

```
[root@e-netsec~]# aureport

Summary Report
======================
Range of time in logs: 12/22/2018 16:25:54.041 -
12/25/2018 11:15:07.407
Selected time for report: 12/22/2018 16:25:54 -
12/25/2018 11:15:07.407
Number of changes in configuration: 16
Number of changes to accounts, groups, or roles: 0
Number of logins: 5
Number of failed logins: 0
Number of authentications: 8
Number of failed authentications: 0
Number of users: 2
Number of terminals: 7
Number of host names: 2
Number of executables: 6
Number of commands: 2
Number of files: 3
```

```
Number of AVC's: 0
Number of MAC events: 5
Number of failed syscalls: 0
Number of anomaly events: 0
Number of responses to anomaly events: 0
Number of crypto events: 272
Number of integrity events: 0
Number of virt events: 0
Number of keys: 5
Number of process IDs: 93
Number of events: 765
```

You can also search the `/var/log/audit.log` file for specific events, for example:

```
[root@e-netsec~]# ausearch --message USER_AUTH
----
time->Sat Oct 17 14:16:12 2020
type=USER_AUTH msg=audit(1602940572.872:124): pid=821 uid=0 auid=4294967295
ses=4294967295 subj=system_u:system_r:local_login_t:s0-s0:c0.c1023
msg='op=PAM:authentication grantors=pam_securetty,pam_unix acct="root"
exe="/usr/bin/login" hostname=centossrv01.e-netsec.int addr=? terminal=tty1 res=success'
----
time->Sat Oct 17 14:16:55 2020
type=USER_AUTH msg=audit(1602940615.908:138): pid=9485 uid=0 auid=4294967295
ses=4294967295 subj=system_u:system_r:sshd_t:s0-s0:c0.c1023
msg='op=PAM:authentication grantors=pam_unix acct="root" exe="/usr/sbin/sshd"
hostname=10.0.0.2 addr=10.0.0.2 terminal=ssh res=success'
----
```

This command will display successful login events. There are many options you can use to search.

Monitor Your Logs

You will also need to monitor your logs closely and keep an eye on them; the best way is to set up a system to receive and process all your logs, and make this system to generate reports based on events you can choose or define.

The easiest way is to use `logwatch` package. `Logwatch` is a powerful and versatile log parser and analyzer. Logwatch was designed to give a unified report of all activity on a server, delivered through the command line or email. `Logwatch` package contains many scripts written in Perl, and it simple parses logs and spits out a simple report.

Install Log watch

```
[root@e-netsec~]# yum install logwatch
```

Note: Logwatch has a set of dependencies; they are Perl modules.

Once the package is installed, it adds a `cron` job:
`/etc/cron.daily/0logwatch`

To configure logwatch you need to edit the following file:

```
[root@e-netsec~]# vi
/usr/share/logwatch/default.conf/logwatch.conf
```

Some parameters you need to configure are:

- `MailTo = sysadmin@e-netsec.net`
- `MailFrom: servera@e-netsec.net`
- `Range = Today`
- `Detail = Medium or high`
- `Service = All`
- `DailyReport = Yes`

This is a fundamental tool; there are some very nice comprehensive tools available to give you very nice reports, including graphs.

Take a look at these monitoring tools; they are very good. They are much more complex to set up than `logwatch`, but it is worth the time and effort.

They give you so many features, cool graphs, can handle multiple types of logging data, ingest multiple weblogs and capture multiple log formats, such as; Windows event logs, Syslog and Networking, and Firewalls.

https://www.elastic.co

https://www.graylog.org

Scan for vulnerabilities

Before you start monitoring your server and put it to production, it is a good idea to scan it for security vulnerabilities, for misconfiguration, and errors with a vulnerability scanner or a similar tool. There are many vulnerability scanners on the market, some free and some are commercial, some are very good and easy to use, some are very complicated to use and expensive

I have used and tested quite a few and particularly like Tenable Nessus, Rapid7, OpenVAS, and a small tool, which I liked a lot called: `lynis`.

`Lynis` is a small and open source security tool; it can help you in auditing your server and give you many ways to make it harder and compliant. It is fast and pretty good and gives so much information; I am amazed by all the information it gives; it checks the OS, the kernel, the boot, the services running, modules loaded, PAM modules, accounts, permissions on files and folders, group ownership, SSH configuration and many more. I am really pleased I came across this security tool, and this is the one I am going to describe how to install and use.

I strongly advise you to make a backup of all files before any modifications.

1. Download and Install Lynix : `https://packages.cisofy.com/`

2. Install Linux dependencies:

`[root@e-netsec~]# yum update ca-certificates curl nss openssl`

3. Create `Lynix` repo (`/etc/yum.repos.d/cisofy-lynis.repo`)

`[root@e-netsec~]# vi (/etc/yum.repos.d/cisofy-lynis.repo`

Add the following lines:

```
[lynis]
name=CISOfy Software - Lynis package
baseurl=https://packages.cisofy.com/community/lynis/r
pm/
enabled=1
gpgkey=https://packages.cisofy.com/keys/cisofy-
software-rpms-public.key
gpgcheck=1
priority=2
```

4. Prepare to Install

```
[root@e-netsec~]# yum makecache fast
[root@e-netsec~]# yum install lynis
```

Once Lynis is installed, you can run it with the following command:

5. Run lynis

```
[root@e-netsec~]# lynis audit system
```

Nagios

Nagios is monitoring software which is widely used; it is very good, stable, it is scalable, reliable, and it is free or open-source.

Many companies use Nagios to monitor not just servers, but the entire network, including network devices, applications, and you name it.

Nagios is easy to install; you can either compile it or install it from the RPMs. Ideally, you would want to compile it to make sure it has not been modified in any way.

Note: This book will not cover the installation of Nagios Core, just the NRPE client.

Installing Nagios NRPE

1. Install Nagios NRPE dependencies

```
[root@e-netsec~]# yum install -y gcc glibc glibc-common
openssl openssl-devel perl wget
```

Note: Once Nagios NRPE has been installed, remove the compiler, for example: `gcc, glibc, glibc-common`

2. Download Nagios `NRPE`

```
[root@e-netsec~]# mkdir /tmp/nrpe
[root@e-netsec~]# cd /tmp/nrpe
[root@e-netsec~]# wget --no-check-certificate -O
nrpe.tar.gz https://github.com/NagiosEnterprises/nrpe/releases/download/nrpe-
4.0.2/nrpe-4.0.2.tar.gz
```

3. Uncompress Nagios NRPE source

```
[root@e-netsec~]# tar xzf nrpe-4.0.2.tar.gz
```

4. Compile NRPE client

```
[root@e-netsec~]# cd /tmp/nrpe/nrpe-4.0.2/
```

```
[root@e-netsec~]# ./configure --enable-command-args
[root@e-netsec~]# make all
```

5. Create user and group

```
[root@e-netsec~]# make install-groups-users
```

6. Install binaries

```
[root@e-netsec~]# make install
```

7. Install Configuration files

```
[root@e-netsec~]# make install-config
```

8. Update Services File /etc/services

```
[root@e-netsec~]# echo >> /etc/services
[root@e-netsec~]# echo '# Nagios services' >> /etc/services
[root@e-netsec~]# echo 'nrpe    5666/tcp' >> /etc/services
```

9. Install services/Daemon

```
[root@e-netsec~]# make install-init
```

10. Configure Firewall

```
[root@e-netsec~]# firewall-cmd -permanent -add-port=5666/tcp
```

Encryption

Talking about security, we also need to discuss encryption. It is unavoidable! What would be the point in going through all this hassle to make our servers more secure if our communication is not secure? If we do not want anyone tapping into our communication channel and reading the information we send across the Internet, reading our emails, collecting our usernames and passwords, then we need to take a step back and make sure this data travelling is not sent in cleartext. The only way is by using technology to encrypt all data sent and received to and from our servers.

The easiest thing to do is to listen to all traffic with a sniffer if we are not using encryption, an attacker will have the upper hand, but on the other hand, if we use encryption, anyone sniffing our traffic won't be able to make sense of the traffic captured, and therefore won't be able to easily decipher it.

There are many different technologies to encrypt data or traffic, and choosing one for your specific case or server is crucial.

We can use SSL/TLS to encrypt data between Browsers/Web Servers and email client/server; we can use SSH to encrypt commands sent to servers, to create a tunnel, we can use VPNs to encrypt traffic across the Internet, and ultimately, we can encrypt data at rest in our servers.

Data is important, and hackers will do anything to get hold of your data; if you value your data and do not want it in the wrong hands, the key is encryption.

HTTPS

Hosting a webserver is no play in the ground; it is a time-consuming task, and keeping a webserver secure is hard. There are many aspects, but one which cannot be neglected is the communication between Client and Server, and normally this is done by using HTTPS instead of HTTP (clear-text).

In order to use HTTPS, you will need to set up your webserver to use an SSL Certificate (my recommendation is to acquire a certificate from a reputable CA). Even if you don't process credit card information through your web site, still important to guarantee to your potential clients, they are reaching the right server, otherwise, anyone can impersonate your server, and your reputation will be at stake.

Configuring Apache to use SSL with a Self-Signed Certificate

1. **Install mod_ssl**
   ```
   [root@e-netsec~]# yum install mod_ssl
   ```

2. **Create certificate folder**
   ```
   [root@e-netsec~]# mkdir /etc/httpd/certificates
   ```

3. **Create Self-Signed certificate**
   ```
   [root@e-netsec~]# openssl req -x509 -nodes -days 365 -newkey
   rsa:2048 -keyout /etc/httpd/certificates/apache.key -out
   /etc/httpd/certificates/apache.crt
   ```

   ```
   Generating a 2048 bit RSA private key
   ...+++
   ...............................+++
   writing new private key to
   '/etc/httpd/certificates/apache.key'
   -----
   You are about to be asked to enter information that will
   be incorporated
   ```

into your certificate request.
What you are about to enter is what is called a
Distinguished Name or a DN.
There are quite a few fields but you can leave some blank
For some fields there will be a default value,
If you enter '.', the field will be left blank.

Country Name (2 letter code) [XX]:GB
State or Province Name (full name) []:Cambridgeshire
Locality Name (eg, city) [Default City]:Cambridge
Organization Name (eg, company) [Default Company Ltd]:e-
NetSec Ltd
Organizational Unit Name (eg, section) []:Security
Common Name (eg, your name or your server's hostname)
[]:lincent01.e-netsec.net
Email Address []:webmaster@e-netsec.net

4. Edit /etc/httpd/conf.d/ssl.conf file

```
[root@e-netsec~]# vi /etc/httpd/conf.d/ssl.conf
```

Add the following lines:

```
SSLCertificateFile /etc/httpd/certificates/apache.crt
SSLCertificateKeyFile /etc/httpd/certificates/apache.key
```

5. Restart Apache

```
[root@e-netsec~]# service httpd restart
```

6. Add Iptables rule to port 443

```
[root@e-netsec~]# vi /etc/sysconfig/iptables
```

Add the following lines:

```
[root@e-netsec~]# firewall-cmd -permanent -add-
port=443/tcp
```

7. Restart firewall

```
[root@e-netsec~]# firewall-cmd -reload
```

8. Testing Certificate

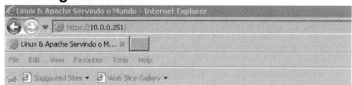

Bem Vindos ao Linux Bem vindos ao nosso servidor Apache Lincent01

VPNs

It is highly recommended to make use of a VPN when connecting your site or office to a remote location or third-party company.

A VPN will protect all traffic from the exit point of your firewall, across the whole Internet to the remote location. A VPN normally is set at the Firewall side, but you can set a tunnel between your Linux server and another server using SSL, SSH, and IPSec (https://www.strongswan.org/) or even the weaker PPTP.

IPsec is stronger and more reliable to use, and it is the one I recommend, but also more time consuming and complex to set up, but once Set up, it requires very little maintenance.

IPSec uses two Phases:

Phase 1

The purpose of IKE phase 1 is to authenticate the IPSec peers and to set up a secure channel between the peers to enable IKE exchanges.

- Authenticates and protects the identities of the IPSec peers
- Negotiates a matching IKE SA policy between peers to protect the IKE exchange
- Performs an authenticated Diffie-Hellman exchange with the result of having matching shared secret keys
- Sets up a secure tunnel to negotiate IKE phase 2 parameters

Phase 2

The purpose of IKE phase 2 is to negotiate IPSec SAs to set up the IPSec tunnel.

- Negotiates IPSec SA parameters protected by an existing IKE SA
- Establishes IPSec security associations
- Periodically renegotiates IPSec SAs to ensure security
- Optionally performs an additional Diffie-Hellman exchange

Encrypting Data at Rest

One can encrypt partitions on your Red Hat Enterprise/Centos Linux 6 server using LUKS (Linux Unified Key Setup-on-disk-format); it is very important to encrypt data at rest on your Linux Server, even on Laptops which can be lost or stolen more easily. LUKS allows multiple user keys to decrypt a master key that is used for the bulk encryption of the partition or volume.

LUKS can give you the following features

- Encrypts entire block devices and is therefore well-suited for protecting the contents of mobile devices such as removable storage media or notebook disk drives.
- The underlying contents of the encrypted block device are arbitrary, making it useful for encrypting swap devices. The encrypting can also be useful with certain databases that use specially formatted block devices for data storage.
- Uses the existing device mapper kernel subsystem.
- Provides passphrase strengthening, which protects against dictionary attaches.
- Allows users to add backup keys or passphrases because LUKS devices contain multiple key slots.

Create a Volume

```
[root@e-netsec~]# pvcreate /dev/sdb
[root@e-netsec~]# vgcreate encrypted /dev/sdb
[root@e-netsec~]# lvcreate -L5G -n lv_encrypted
encrypted
```

Encrypting Your Volume

```
[root@e-netsec~]# fdisk -l | grep /dev/mapper/
```

```
[root@e-netsec~]# cryptsetup -y -v luksFormat
/dev/mapper/encrypted-lv_encrypted
[root@e-netsec~]# blkid | grep LUKS
[root@e-netsec~]# cryptsetup luksOpen
/dev/mapper/encrypted-lv_encrypted cryptData
[root@e-netsec~]# cryptsetup -v status cryptData
[root@e-netsec~]# shred -v -n1 /dev/mapper/cryptData
[root@e-netsec~]# mkfs.ext4 /dev/mapper/cryptData
[root@e-netsec~]# mount /dev/mapper/cryptData
/opt/encrypted/
```

Graphing trends

Graphs are a very useful means to visualize or illustrate relationships in the data. The objective of creating a graph is to show specific data which are too great and complicated in an easy and comprehensive visual way.

Graphing trends are important because you can quickly visualize patterns that otherwise would take a very long time to read or understand. It can show you numerous things, such as;

For example, An IP address is attempting the same username multiple times.
You are getting too many errors in accessing a resource; too much traffic is going through a specific Network port and many more.

So it is also important to have a system which collects all your data, logs, error logs, access logs, firewall logs, network traffic, Syslog data, and you name it and centralize it and process this data, so you can quickly observe certain patterns and quickly be alerted of problems.

Luckily there is such a system, and it is pretty good at what it does; graphing data. "Grafana allows you to query, visualize, alert on, and understand your metrics no matter where they are stored. Create, explore, and share dashboards with your team and foster a data-driven culture."

I recommend Grafana. You can download it from Grafana's website at
`https://grafana.com/grafana`

How to install Grafana

1. Yum install Grafana

```
[root@e-netsec~]# yum install https://s3-us-west-
2.amazonaws.com/grafana-releases/release/grafana-6.2.2-
1.x86_64.rpm
```

2. Start Grafana Server

```
[root@e-netsec~]# systemctl enable grafana-server
[root@e-netsec~]# systemctl start grafana-server
```

3. Open your browser and explore Grafana

http://10.0.0.30:3000
Note: Don't forget to add an firewall rule to allow port 3000.

4. Type in username and password:
admin/admin

Note: you should change the admin password right away.

The main grafana's configuration file is /etc/grafana/grafana.ini. Once
you have logged into Grafana, you should see a screen similar to the
one below:

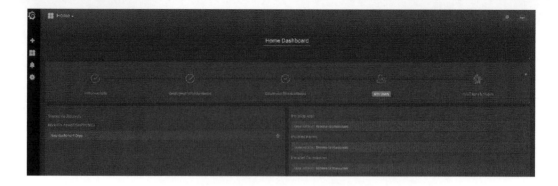

It is pretty much blank, and your task is to configure, add data sources, and start graphing your data.

5. Install Server-side image rendering

```
[root@e-netsec~]# vi /etc/yum.repos/grafana.repo
```

Add:

```
[grafana]
name=grafana
baseurl=https://packagecloud.io/grafana/stable/el/7/$basearch
repo_gpgcheck=1
enabled=1
gpgcheck=1
gpgkey=https://packagecloud.io/gpg.key
https://grafanarel.s3.amazonaws.com/RPM-GPG-KEY-grafana
sslverify=1
sslcacert=/etc/pki/tls/certs/ca-bundle.crt
```

6. Install Rendering packages

```
[root@e-netsec~]# yum install fontconfig freetype*
urw-fonts
```

7. Install InfluxDB Database

```
[root@e-netsec~]# vi /etc/yum.repos.d/influxdb.repo
```

Add the following content:

```
[influxdb]
name = InfluxDB Repository - RHEL \$releasever
baseurl = https://repos.influxdata.com/rhel/\$releasever/\$basearch/stable
enabled = 1
gpgcheck = 1
gpgkey = https://repos.influxdata.com/influxdb.key
```

8. Update cache and install InfluxDB

```
[root@e-netsec~]# yum makecache fast

[root@e-netsec~]# yum install influxdb
```

9. Create user/database

```
[root@e-netsec~]# influx

Connected to http://localhost:8086 version 1.7.2
InfluxDB shell version: 1.7.2
Enter an InfluxQL query
> CREATE USER admin WITH PASSWORD 'password' WITH ALL
PRIVILEGES

[root@e-netsec~]# influx -username admin -password
"password"

Connected to http://localhost:8086 version 1.7.2
InfluxDB shell version: 1.7.2
Enter an InfluxQL query
> SHOW USERS
user   admin
----   -----
admin true
> SHOW DATABASES
name: databases
name
----
_internal
```

```
> CREATE DATABASE grafana
> GRANT ALL PRIVILEGES TO admin
```

Create a Data Source

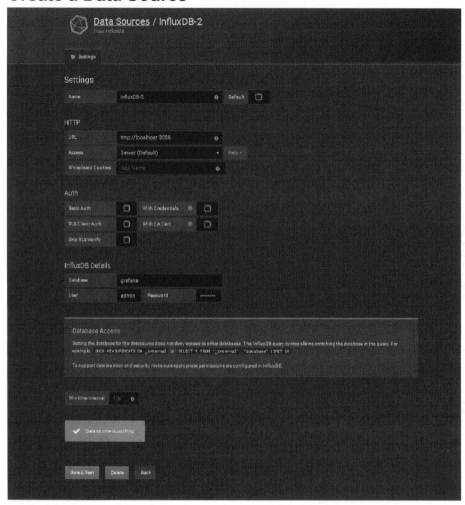

Create a Dashboard

1. Click on the arrow down new Home, at the top, left hand

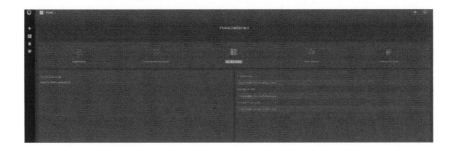

2. Click on "New dashboard."

3. You can choose one of the options below. Let's create a graph

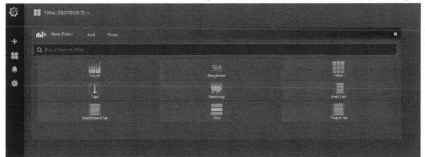

4. Edit the graph created. Click on [Panel Title], the [Edit]

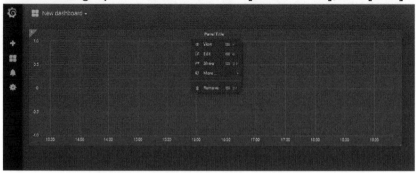

5. Select your Data Source.
   In my case, my Data Source is "InfluxDB-2", then I chose [-Grafana-] metric.

Grafana Metric

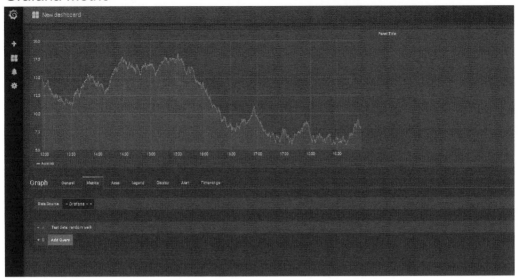

Once your `grafana` is up and running, it is up to you and your creativity to graph any data you want. You can graph metrics from your servers, such as:

- Load
- Network Traffic
- CPU Load
- Application memory usage
- SWAP
- Disk Space
- Web pages hits

You will never stop adding new graphs; time, and time again, I find myself adding new ones. It helps me in troubleshooting problems in identifying bottlenecks, offending IPs, and many more.

Elastic Search

Elastic search is a search engine based on the Lucene library. It provides a distributed, multitenant-capable full-text search engine with an HTTP web interface and schema-free JSON documents. According to the DB-Engines ranking, Elastic search is the most popular enterprise search engine, it is flexible, scalable, distributed, and you can use for a multitude of data.

The idea is to set elastic search on a server and through all your data at it and let it process it and create events to search for errors, connections denied, rejected, login failed, and any event which concerns you.
This is a pretty powerful solution and will help in collecting all your data and make sense of it, searching for patterns.

Miscellaneous

This part of this book brings together many HOWTOs, which I chose to describe to you. I hope they can help you in many ways.

How To Disable Local Login for specific users

To control this option, allow a user to log in via SSH, and deny the same user access via the console, we need to edit the file: /etc/security/access.conf

```
[root@e-netsec~]# vi /etc/security/access.conf
```

Add the user name you wish to deny access to your server, for example:

- : ALLEXCEPT root:tty1 tty2 tty3 tty4 tty5 tty6 LOCAL

Configuring PAM modules

```
[root@e-netsec~]# cd /etc/pam.d
```

```
[root@e-netsec~]# vi login
```

Add the Line Below at the top:

```
account     required     pam_access.so
```

```
[root@e-netsec~]# vi sshd
```

```
account     required     pam_access.so
```

```
[root@e-netsec~]# vi password-auth
```

Add the Line Below at the top:

```
account      required       pam_access.so
```

Edit /etc/ssh/sshd_config

```
[root@e-netsec~]# vi /etc/ssh/sshd_config
```

```
UsePAM yes
```

How To Install Nagios using yum

Install Epel repo
```
[root@e-netsec~]# yum install epel-release.noarch
```

Install Nagios Server
```
[root@e-netsec~]# yum install -y nagios nagios-devel
nagios-plugins* gd gd-devel httpd php gcc glibc glibc-
common openssl
```

Set Nagios Admin Password
```
[root@e-netsec~]# htpasswd -c /etc/nagios/passwd
nagiosadmin
```

Set Nagios to start at boot time
```
[root@e-netsec~]# systemctl enable httpd
[root@e-netsec~]# systemctl enable nagios
```

Install Nagios Client (NRPE)
```
[root@e-netsec~]# yum install nrpe nagios-plugins-all
```

Configure Nagios Client (NRPE)
```
[root@e-netsec~]# vi /etc/nagios/nrpe.cfg
```

Set NRPE Options
```
allowed_hosts=127.0.0.1, 192.168.1.110
```

```
command[check_users]=/usr/lib64/nagios/plugins/check_us
ers -w 5 -c 10
command[check_load]=/usr/lib64/nagios/plugins/check_loa
d -w 15,10,5 -c 30,25,20
command[check_hda1]=/usr/lib64/nagios/plugins/check_dis
k -w 20% -c 10% -p /dev/hda1
command[check_zombie_procs]=/usr/lib64/nagios/plugins/c
heck_procs -w 5 -c 10 -s Z
command[check_total_procs]=/usr/lib64/nagios/plugins/ch
eck_procs -w 150 -c 200

[root@e-netsec~]# systemctl enable nrpe
```

How to check if Your Domain is blacklisted

It is very important to keep an eye on what is going on throughout your network.   It is fundamental to know what is happening and has happened. Keeping track of your domains and/if they are blacklisted is key in maintaining your system's health and in good order.
There is a small utility which does this really well, it is called: Blacklist-check

I strongly advise you to make a backup of all files, prior to any modifications.

Download and Install Blacklist-check

```
[root@e-netsec~]# cd /usr/local/bin
[root@e-netsec~]# wget
https://raw.githubusercontent.com/adionditsak/blacklist
-check-unix-linux-utility/master/bl

[root@e-netsec~]# mv bl blacklist-check

[root@e-netsec~]# chmod 755 blacklist-check
```

```
[root@e-netsec~]# ./blacklist-check e-netsec.net
```

Automate Blacklist-check

```
[root@e-netsec~]# crontab -e
```

Add:

```
0 23 * * sun "/usr/local/bin/blacklist-check domain"
```

Download BlackList
```
[root@e-netsec~]# wget
```

Apache access Log

I suggest checking your Apache's `/var/log/httpd/access_log` periodically, inspecting it for multiple IP connections, referrers, 404 responses etc.

Check for referrers

```
[root@e-netsec~]# awk '{print $11}'
/var/log/httpd/access_log | sort -u
```

Check for 404 Errors

```
[root@e-netsec~]# awk '$9==404 {print $7}'
/var/log/httpd/access_log
```

Count IPs

```
[root@e-netsec~]# cat /var/log/httpd/access_log |cut -d
' ' -f 1 |sort
```

```
[root@e-netsec~]# cat /var/log/httpd/access_log |awk '{print $1}' |sort
|uniq -c |sort -n |tail
```

Check most viewed pages

```
[root@e-netsec~]# awk '{print $7}' /var/log/httpd/access_log |cut -d? -
f1|sort|uniq -c|sort -nk1|tail -n10
```

Check IPs and most viewed pages

```
[root@e-netsec~]# awk '{print $1,$7}'
/var/log/httpd/access_log | cut -d? -f1 | sort | uniq -
c |sort -nr
```

How to Set-up SpamAssassin

Spamassassin is a SPAM filtering tool for Linux and it works really well together with Postfix. I will describe below how to install it and configure it to be invoked by Postfix and protect your server against Unsolicited Emails.

This is very useful tool in the battle to keep your Network and your server and client's safety.

Install SpamAssassin

1. Install SpamAssassin
```
[root@e-netsec~]# yum search spamassassin
```

```
[root@e-netsec~]# yum install spamassassin evolution-
spamassassin.x86_64 spamassassin-iXhash2.noarc
```

2. Config Spamassassin
```
[root@e-netsec~]# vi /etc/mail/spamassassin/local.cf
```

Add the following lines:

```
required_hits 5.0
report_safe 0
required_score 5
```

```
rewrite_header Subject !!!SPAM!!!
```

Add user/Group

```
[root@e-netsec~]# groupadd spamd
[root@e-netsec~]# useradd -g spamd -s /bin/false -d
/var/log/spamassassin spamd
[root@e-netsec~]# chown spamd:spamd /var/log/spamassassin
```

Configure Postfix

```
[root@e-netsec~]# vi /etc/postfix/master.cf
```

Comment the following line

```
# smtp      inet  n   -   n   -   -   smtpd
```

Add the following line:

```
smtp inet n - n - - smtpd -o content_filter=spamassassin
```

On the Same file, add the line below at the bottom

```
spamassassin unix - n n - - pipe flags=R user=spamd
argv=/usr/bin/spamc -e /usr/sbin/sendmail -oi -f ${sender}
${recipient}
```

Restart SpamAssassin and Postfix

```
[root@e-netsec~]# systemctl status spamassassin
[root@e-netsec~]# systemctl enable spamassassin
[root@e-netsec~]# systemctl start spamassassin
```

How To Install and configure ClamAV

Having a good Antivirus installed is fundamental for any basic security. This step should be at the top of every security list. I am amazed how many users and sysadmins remove antiviruses justifying it slow down their PC or Server.

1. Download the Epel repository package

```
 [root@e-netsec~]# yum search epel
Last metadata expiration check: 2:11:30 ago on Mon 26
Oct 2020 06:53:56 GMT.
=============== Name Matched: epel ====================
epel-release.noarch : Extra Packages for Enterprise Linux
repository configuration


[root@e-netsec~]# yum install epel-release.noarch
```

2. Download and Install ClamAV

```
[root@e-netsec~]# yum search clamav
clamav.x86_64
clamav-filesystem.noarch
clamav-unofficial-sigs.noarch
clamav-lib.x86_64
clamav-data.noarch
clamav-devel.x86_64
clamav-milter.x86_64
clamav-update.x86_64


[root@e-netsec~]# yum install clamav.x86_64 clamav-
filesystem.noarch clamav-lib.x86_64 clamav-data.noarch
clamav-update.x86_64
```

3. Update Virus Definition

```
[root@e-netsec~]# /usr/bin/freshclam
```

Note: The Clamav-update package installs /usr/bin/freshclam and /etc/freshclam.conf.

4. Edit `/etc/freshclam.conf`.

Uncomment the following lines:

##
Example config file for freshclam
Please read the freshclam.conf(5) manual before editing this file.
##
DatabaseDirectory /var/lib/clamav
UpdateLogFile /var/log/freshclam.log
LogFileMaxSize 2M
LogTime yes
LogVerbose yes
LogSyslog yes
LogRotate yes

Note: Save the file and exit

5. Add freshclam to crontab

```
[root@e-netsec~]# crontab -e
# Update ClamAV vírus definition
0 10 * * * /usr/bin/freshclam
```

6. Automating scans

```
[root@e-netsec~]# crontab -e
# Antivirus scan
0 11 * * * /usr/bin/clamscan --detect-pua -i -r /u01 --
log="$HOME/.clamtk/history/$(date +\%b-\%d-\%Y).log" 2>/dev/null
```

HOW TO SSH Port Knocking

Port Knocking is yet another way to secure your server from unauthorized users. Port Knocking works by opening ports on the `iptables` firewall by generating a connection attempt on a set of pre-defined closed ports. Once a correct sequence of connection attempts is received by port knocking (20 sec set), the `iptables` will open the port that was previously closed. Port knocking is used to defend your Linux server against port scanners. Changing your default `ssh` port is not a secure method to protect your server, because the attacker often uses a port scanner to do automated scans for open ports before attacking a server. So the port knocking is another layer to secure your `ssh` server.

For example, if you want to set up port knocking for port 22, this port will only be open when you request to the port 2222, 3333, 4444 in sequence (within 20 seconds). When you complete the sequence correctly the `iptables` will open the port 22 for you.

It is great because it hides your server and the sequence number is only known by you and whomever you share it with.

1. Download Port Knocking Package
```
[root@e-netsec~]# cd /usr/local/src
[root@e-netsec~]# wget
https://li.nux.ro/download/nux/dextop/el7Server/x86_64/knock-
server-0.7-2.el7.nux.x86_64.rpm
```

2. Download Port Knocking dependencies
```
[root@e-netsec~]# yum install libpcap-devel.x86_64
libpcap.x86_64 -y
```

3. Install Port Knocking package
```
[root@e-netsec~]# rpm -Uvh knock-server-0.7-
2.el7.nux.x86_64.rpm -y
```

4. Edit /etc/sysconfig/iptables

and remove the following lines:

```
firewall-cmd -zone=public -remove-service=ssh --
permanent
```

5. Restart `firewall`

```
[root@e-netsec~]# firewall-cmd --reload
```

6. Edit /etc/sysconfig/knockd

Add the following line:
```
START_KNOCKD=1
```

7. Configure /etc/knockd.conf
Add the following lines:

```
[options]
  UseSyslog
  logfile = /var/log/knockd.log

[opencloseSSH]
  sequence      = 2222,3333,4444
  seq_timeout   = 20
  tcpflags      = syn
  start_command = /bin/firewall-cmd --zone=public
    --add-rich-rule="rule family="ipv4" source address="%IP%"
    service name="ssh" accept"


[closeSSH]
  sequence        = 2222,3333,4444
  seq_timeout     = 20
  command         = /bin/firewall-cmd --zone=public
    --remove-rich-rule="rule family="ipv4" source
    address="%IP%" service name="ssh" accept"
```

```
        tcpflags          = syn
```

Glossary

Protocol – It is a pre-defined set of rules, which helps in stablishing a communication between two disparate systems.

SSH – **Secure Shell** is a secure protocol which allows one to remotely connect to a Linux/Unix Server or Client and run commands as if you were physically logged on. It uses strong encryption and therefore is very secure. It uses TCP port 22.

RDP – **Remote Desktop Protocol** is a protocol developed by Microsoft, which provides a user with a graphical interface to connect to another computer running Windows over a network connection. It uses TCP port 3389.

VPN – **Virtual Private Network** is a method to connect to a private network over a public Internet using public infrastructure, and become part of the local Network. VPN uses encryption and there are different types of VPNs.

SMTP – **Simple Mail Transfer Protocol** is a protocol used to transfer email from a client to a server or from a server to another server. It uses TCP port 25 for clear text insecure and TCP port 587 for secured with encryption.

IMAP – **Internet Message Access Protocol** is a protocol used by email clients to check emails on a remote server and allow you to use them as if they were stored locally on your PC. It uses TCP port 143 for clear text insecure and 993 for secured with encryption.

POP3 – **Post Office Protocol** is a protocol used by email clients to transfer email from the local PC to the remote server. It uses TCP port 110 for clear text insecure and TCP port 995 for secure with encryption.

PHISHING – It is the attempt to obtain sensitive information such as usernames, passwords, and credit card details (and, indirectly, money), often for malicious reasons, by disguising as a trustworthy entity in an electronic communication. The word is a neologism created as a homophone of *fishing* due to the similarity of using bait in an attempt to catch a victim.

Firewall – A Firewall is software or hardware or a combination of both, which helps in preventing unauthorised connections to and from Networks or servers, by allowing or denying connection to services or applications hosted within a server, based on TCP ports and IP addresses. The firewall looks at the network traffic and based where it is coming from and/or going to, the firewall makes decisions and either let the packets go or just drop it.

RSA Key – Is a private **key** based on **RSA** algorithm. Private **Key** is used for authentication and a symmetric **key** exchange during establishment of an SSL/TLS session. It is a part of the public **key** infrastructure that is generally used in case of SSL certificates.

Second Factor Authentication – **Two Factor Authentication**, also known as 2FA, **two step** verification or TFA (as an acronym), is an extra layer of security that is known as "multi **factor authentication**" that requires not only a password and username but also something that only, and only, that user has on them, i.e. a piece of information only they.

Google Authenticator – It is a software token that implements two-step verification services using the Time-based One-time Password Algorithm (TOTP) and HMAC-based One-time Password Algorithm (HOTP), for authenticating users of mobile applications by **Google**.

HTTP – Hyper Text Transfer protocol is a protocol/application used for collaboration, media information, data communication over the web and it is the basis for the WWW (World Wide Web), as with the other protocols, it has the clear text version and the encrypted secure version using HTTPS over SSL. It uses TCP port 80 for the clear text version and 443 for the encrypted version.

FTP – File Transfer Protocol is protocol used by users/clients to transfer (upload/download) files to and from remote servers. As with all protocols, there is a clear text version and a more secure version, which uses encryption, it is called FTPS. It uses two TCP ports 20 and 21 for clear text and 990 for secure encrypted version.

Telnet – Is a protocol/program which allows one to connect remotely to another terminal or computer and execute commands remotely. Telnet is clear text and is extremely insecure and it is pretty much obsolete now a days. It listens on TCP port 23, as with most protocols and programs there is a secure version SSH, avoid using Telnet, it is very insecure as all traffic can be captured and read by anyone.

Jail breaking – is the process of removing software restrictions imposed by Apple on their Operating system "IOS". This is done by using some modified kernel software. Jailbreaking permits **root access** to Apple operating system iOS. This allows downloading and installation of additional applications, extensions, and themes that are unavailable through the official **Apple App Store** and potentially insecure.

UPnP - Universal Plug and Play is a set of networking protocols that permits networked devices, such as personal computers, printers, Internet gateways, Wi-Fi access points and mobile devices to seamlessly discover each other's presence on the Network and establish functional network services for data sharing.

Dynamic DNS - DDNS or DynDNS is a method of automatically updating a name server in the Domain Name System, often in real time. It is useful and helpful for Internet connections where the IP is assigned by DHCP and changes constantly i.e. broadband, cable modem etc., so the Dynamic DNS automatic updates the IP address.

DHCP – Dynamic Host Configuration Protocol is a protocol used by client and servers to automatically assign IP addresses to clients. There are two parts of it, the client side and the server side. The client requests IPs and the server serves IPs to the client. It is very useful if you have many computers and need to assign IPs to all of them, having a mechanism to automate this task is very important.

MAC Address – Media Access Control is a 48 bit HEX decimal number written to all Ethernet Network Cards and WIFI cards as well. This number helps uniquely identifying each NIC on a network.

SSID – It is a case sensitive, 32 alphanumeric character unique identifier attached to the header of packets sent over a wireless local-area network (WLAN). It is the name of your WIFI network, the one your client device sees and connects to on a WIFI network.

WEP - Wired Equivalent Privacy is a security protocol, specified in the IEEE Wireless Fidelity (Wi-Fi) standard, 802.11b, that is designed to provide a wireless local area network (WLAN) with a level of security and privacy comparable to what is usually expected of a wired LAN.

WAP - Wireless Application Protocol is a technical standard for accessing information over a mobile wireless network. A **WAP** browser is a web browser for mobile devices such as mobile phones that uses the protocol.

UAC - User Account Control is a security feature of Windows which helps prevent unauthorized changes to the operating system. These changes can be initiated by applications, users, viruses or other forms of malware. User Account Control makes sure certain changes are made only with approval from the administrator. If the changes are not approved by the administrator, they are not executed, and Windows remains unchanged. It is as if nothing happened. UAC was first made available for Windows Vista, and since then it was improved with each new version of Windows.

PSK – Pre-Shared Key is a pre-defined password used by WIFI routers to allow access to its SSID, it can be 64 bit long. Whenever you connect to an SSID provided by an Access Point, you will be prompted to provide a password or pre-share key.

SSL – Secure Sockets Layer is the standard security technology for establishing an encrypted link between a web server and a browser. This link ensures that all data passed between the web server and browsers remain private and integral.

BIOS – Basic Input Output System For IBM PC compatible computers compatible computers, **PC BIOS**, is non-volatile firmware used to perform hardware initialization during the booting process (power-on startup), and to provide runtime services for operating systems and programs. The BIOS firmware comes pre-installed on a personal computer's system board, and it is the first software run when powered on. The name originates from the Basic Input/Output System used in the CP/M operating system in 1975. Originally proprietary to the IBM PC, the BIOS has been reverse engineered by companies looking to create compatible systems.

AES – The **Advanced Encryption Standard** (**AES**), also known by its original name **Rijndael,** is a specification for the encryption of electronic data established by the U.S. National Institute of Standards and Technology (NIST) in 2001.

AES is a subset of the Rijndael cipher developed by two Belgian cryptographers; Vincent Rijmen and Joan Daemen, who submitted a proposal to NIST during the AES selection process. Rijndael is a family of ciphers with different key and block sizes.

BitLocker – is a full disk encryption feature included with Windows Vista and later. It is designed to protect data by providing encryption for entire volumes. By default it uses the AES encryption algorithm in cipher block chaining (CBC) or XTS mode with a 128-bit or 256-bit key.

Zero Day Attacks - Is vulnerability refers to a hole in software that is unknown to the vendor. This security hole is then exploited by hackers before the vendor becomes aware and hurries to fix it.